the
wide-eyed
wonder
years

the
wide-eyed
wonder
years

a mommy guide
to the preschool daze

LORILEE CRAKER

Grand Rapids, Michigan

© 2006 by Lorilee Craker

Published by Fleming H. Revell
a division of Baker Publishing Group
P.O. Box 6287, Grand Rapids, MI 49516-6287

Printed in the United States of America

Library of Congress Cataloging-in-Publication Data
Craker, Lorilee.
    The wide-eyed wonder years : a mommy guide to the preschool daze / Lorilee Craker.
        p.   cm.
    Includes bibliographical references.
    ISBN 0-8007-3064-X (pbk.)
    1. Preschool children. 2. Preschool children—Anecdotes. 3. Child rearing. 4. Parent and child. I. Title.
HQ774.5.C74 2006
305.233—dc22   2005028400

Unless otherwise indicated, Scripture is taken from the HOLY BIBLE, NEW INTERNATIONAL VERSION®. NIV®. Copyright © 1973, 1978, 1984 by International Bible Society. Used by permission of Zondervan. All rights reserved.

Scripture marked KJV is taken from the King James Version of the Bible.

To Phoebe Min-Ju Jayne,
my bright, shining star;
shine like stars in the universe

Contents

INTRODUCTION

THE KID IS wearing his bathing suit in January, glaring at the glob of broccoli on his plate, asking the kinds of questions—in public—that make your ears turn bright red: he's a preschooler, and it shows.

Gone are the baby days of yore, when his vocabulary consisted of "uh-oh" and "kitty." Now his constant queries about everything under the sun—and including the sun—are making you (almost) wistful for his toddlerhood, when you asked him to "use his words" about a million times. Actually, you're not sure if the pet snail is a girl, if the moon is fuzzy, or if the mailman uses the potty (well, that's a no-brainer, at least—you think). But it falls upon you on a regular basis to cough up a brilliant answer. He talks a mile a minute unless, of course, he's in public, where he becomes mute and stony faced. That is, he's shy other than when he has a burning question, like the time he asked the seventy-year-old visiting pastor if he was wearing underwear. Well, he wanted to know!

Preschoolers. They don't get the adoration given to babies, and their rap sheets aren't nearly as long as those of intractable toddlers, but three-, four-, and five-year-olds are their own animals. And according to development experts, this two or two-and-a-half-year period is absolutely foundational to their entire lives. *The Focus on the Family Complete Book of Baby and Child Care* calls the preschool years "an extraordinary period." The authors write, "For a number of reasons, the two years leading to the fifth birthday are a unique and critical period, during which you can shape the entire gamut of your child's attitudes and understanding."[1] Wow. Who knew?

Actually, I'm not surprised. The preschool years were, thus far, my favorite era with my older son, Jonah, who is now seven. And because we had such a blast with Jonah, I was excited for Ezra to bloom into one of those hilarious, oh-so-silly sweethearts too.

Why am I so pumped up about preschoolers? These miniature people have great verbal skills; the only problem is they say anything and everything they are thinking—out loud! Sometimes their little blurts are embarrassing (much more on this later), and other times what comes out of their mouths is cute, precocious, or odd.

"Mommy, potatoes are very quiet," my four-year-old remarked this morning as I was buckling him in his car seat.

I agreed—"Yes, Ez, potatoes are quiet"—because what else can be said?

Last week he asked me one of a million or so questions burning in his boy bosom: "Mommy, what's a disco ball?"

Where do they get this stuff? You just never know what these funny, quirky creatures are going to say.

The Wide-Eyed Wonder Years reveals the shine and brilliance of these amazing and precious years in your child's life. You'll discover incredible opportunities to teach, disciple, enjoy, and grow closer than ever to your little ones. Three-, four-, and five-year-olds *are* wide eyed and full of wonder. Perhaps at no other time in childhood are they as impressionable and curious as this! Moms, these are the salad days of child rearing. You aren't spending all your time putting out fires—as you are with toddlers—yet you still have copious amounts of quality time to spend nurturing and investing in your pint-sized wunderkind.

Of course, every phase of growing up has its bumps to climb on. Believe me, I have climbed some bumps with my wild and woolly boys! It's still bumpy around here most days. Ezra's four, right at the peak of his wide-eyed wonder years, and all the research and tips from fellow moms I collected for this book I applied to my daily life with him. Who are these mommies in the trenches? Meet my preschool panel, a group of savvy, witty chicks who answered my questions and gave me so much great material about their own rascals. Throughout the book, you'll hear from Alanna, Jen T., Jen P., Brenna, Christy, Alicia, Mary Jo, Cheryl, Ann, Sharon, Johana, Mary, Jodi, Amy, and Kim—the main coconspirators in this two-hundred-page attempt to comprehend small children and their quirks.

Together we've considered mysteries such as: Why do three-year-olds behave like overgrown toddlers some days? How come my four-year-old is terrified of "monsters," and

11

my seven-year-old is so over that? Is it possible to pave the way for a smoother transition to preschool (and unclamp the kid from my leg)?

These are the questions that pop up with my Ez the Pez and the tykes of my preschool panel. Chances are good that you have raised similar queries yourself. In finding answers and solutions to my preschool puzzles, hopefully I've found some for you too.

Here's just a sampling of the topics covered within these pages:

Getting kids to share and not kill each other: the miracle "cure."

Soothing your little one's fear of the dark and monsters: banish the boogeyman for good.

Oh-so-picky eating: why three-year-olds like only five foods, and how to expand their menu beyond PB&J.

Best playtimes for preschoolers: the wondrous benefits of doll play, wooden trains, and dressing up.

And a few subjects just for you:

Mommy body image: how to like the skin you're in.

How to keep the home fires burning: Mom and Dad got it going *on*.

Curious, capricious, and imaginative, your preschooler straddles the worlds of babyhood and childhood. Drawing on my own life with my boys, interviews with experts, and loads of research, I'm giving you the 411 on this fantastic phase and a deeper glimpse at your peerless preschooler's experience. Here's hoping that between the funny stories, the road-tested tips, and the hard-won wisdom from me and my fellow mom contributors, you can make the most of the often amusing, sometimes maddening, wide-eyed wonder years of your precious, amazing child.

1

"I CAN'T BELIEVE HE SAID THAT!"

Buttoning your preschooler's embarrassing blurts

THIS SUMMER, EZRA said to my dear friend from high school, whom I hadn't seen in almost six years, "Why are you so fat? Do you eat too much junk food?" I wanted to be vaporized by aliens. My friend, who is not "so fat" at all, laughed it off gamely, joking with the little shyster. But I was utterly mortified.

Preschoolers! They have the language skills to chat up a storm yet have absolutely no inhibitions. They will poke you in an elevator and whisper loudly, "Mommy, that lady has a mustache!" They will lift up your skirt in public and tell the guy next to you that you are wearing pretty underwear. They will confide in your pastor after church that—giggle, giggle—Mommy sometimes pees when she sneezes!

You've no doubt heard these kinds of blurts from your offspring because, well, 99 percent of kids this age simply have no couth. Preschoolers are bound to point out anything that's new or striking to them. This means Great-Aunt Beulah, with her five o'clock shadow, is in trouble—and so are you.

Pint-Sized Pundits Call It Like They See It

Amy was in some hot water when a certain little pitcher with big ears blabbed a private conversation, out of context, about her *mother-in-law*. (I bet you're shuddering, and you haven't even heard the story yet!)

My daughter informed my in-laws that "Mommy did not want to ever go to their house again." She had overheard a discussion my husband and I had when we returned home from a weekend away after traveling with my newborn and three-year-old. My mother-in-law had invited us over for dinner and we hadn't been home all weekend, and I did not want to pack up the kids for yet another night out of the house. Needless to say, her blurt did not go over well.

Pint-sized pundits each one, preschoolers call it like they see it, which is why Jen T.'s Gabbi told someone, "You *stink*! You need a mint!" and Christy's daughter pointed to a paraplegic in a grocery store, broadcasting the words, "Look, Mommy, that man has no legs. Why?"

Truly, the blurters among us have no social filters, and this fact renders them cluelessly rude even though their remarks aren't meant to hurt or malign anyone. Most people

16

do understand that our little blabbermouths are innocent, but when they speak out of turn, it can be embarrassing, right?

The King of Blurts

My son Jonah was perhaps the king of blurts when he was three, four, and five. He was very verbal and said the first thing that popped into his little towhead. The Easter that he was four, I came downstairs wearing a new spiffy springtime ensemble he had never seen before. "Mommy looks pretty!" he said to my husband, Doyle. "Why does she?"

Once Jonah watched a seventy-something Dutch locksmith change the locks on our front door. I'm not sure if he spotted a plumber's backside situation or if he was just jazzed about getting some new Spider-Man skivvies, but after watching the man finagle with the lock for a while, he just came out with it: "Are you wearing underwear?" Later I heard from a mutual friend that our locksmith had never in all his years of performing his services heard such a question!

Of course, this situation was a far sight better than one mom's plight with her yakky preschooler. The only boy in a family of four sisters, little Paul was very proud of and fascinated by his male member, a rarity in that household. Naturally, he wanted to know who else in his universe had such a wonder attached to their bodies. So for a few weeks, he asked people wherever he went, "Do you have a penis?" Oy!

17

Political Correctness Is Not a Preschooler's Strong Suit

Often, kids will question something they aren't used to seeing, like Great-Aunt Beulah's furry chin. When it comes to pointing out differences in skin color, comments can get quite politically *in*correct.

"Mommy, she's not black!" Jonah exclaimed upon seeing the receptionist at the doctor's office. "Um, no, she's not," I said. I knew what Jonah was thinking: Dr. Addy, his pediatrician, is African, and Jonah was anticipating a smiling woman with black skin.

I managed to distract him from this train of thought with some toys and breathed a sigh of relief that he hadn't continued his line of questioning. (I could picture him commenting on the skin color of every person sitting in the waiting room.)

Of course, life with a preschooler is rarely that simple. A little while later, when Dr. Addy was examining Jonah at close range, the Mouth spoke again: "She's got black ears, Mom!" Oh my. With someone less congenial—and less accustomed to the out-loud blurts of small children—the situation could have become awkward. Thankfully, Dr. Addy chuckled and didn't miss a beat with the old tongue depressor routine. "Yes, you noticed, did you," she said, smiling at Jonah.

Sometimes, the target of such innocent but potentially upsetting remarks is less understanding. Or perhaps they have a handicap, in which case they may not welcome attention drawn to them. We had two encounters with dwarfs when Jonah was small, one positive and one negative. The

18

second guy did not appreciate one bit my little boy's calling out, "Look how tiny that man is!" Gulp.

Damage Control for When the Mouth Strikes

We don't know precisely when the Mouth will strike, but when it does, we can do a few things to help finesse the child's social skills:

In the moment, casually answer your child's blurt. "Yes, God made people of all sizes, didn't he?" (Or, to comment on Great-Auntie's beard: "Oh, you're such a silly boy." The word "silly" can bail you out of numerous situations. Do apologize to the offended party, lightly, if you feel it's appropriate at the moment. "I'm sorry about that! He's just at that age where he says the craziest things!") Later, tell Blabby you know he didn't mean to hurt the dwarf's feelings, but when we stare or ask loud questions it might make the person feel bad (or in Aunt Beulah's case, inspire her to check into electrolysis).

Don't gasp and sputter and force your child to apologize. This will only draw more attention to the unsavory situation. And the Mouth will be totally confused.

If your child infrequently has the opportunity to see people of other races, buy some picture books and talk about how beautiful different colors of skin are. She may excitedly point out the next person of a different color she sees, in which case you could again apply a

19

light touch—"Yes, I see that!"—and later follow up
with another speech about pointing.

FUN THINGS

A note about "Fun Things." Since preschoolers are
so funny (sometimes not at the moment but later),
and because occasionally all we can do is laugh,
I'm ending each chapter of this book with "Fun
Things." It's a hodgepodge of preschool blurts,
humorous lists, and other amusing bits and pieces
to wrap things up with a smile.

Can You Believe She Said That?

When we brought our now five-month-old home, Grace
asked, "What's wrong with his pee-pee butt, Mom?" (That's
what she's been naming her parts—a pee-pee butt and a
poopy butt.) We tried to explain that boys have a penis. For a
while we thought she got it until one day when friends were
over and I was changing Gabe's diaper after his circumcision.
Grace said, "Yeah, Gabe's got a boo-boo on his peanut
because he's a boy." I about lost it then!—**Christy**

On Father's Day, Elana had a tummy ache, and when her
father ran her to the bathroom, they didn't quite make it and
she threw up all over his shirt. "Mommy," she said, "I threw
Daddy up!"—**Kim**

20

2

TO SHARE IS HUMAN

Doing so without Mommy telling you to is divine!

"Get Your Paws off My Stuff!"

"Mom! Ezra keeps grabbing my new Bionicle!" Jonah's frustration was bubbling, and I could tell pretty soon they were gonna have a little tussle. OK, maybe more like fists were going to fly, tears were going to flow, and all manner of mayhem and discord would bust loose from the moorings of our quasi-peaceful home.

Of course I was on the phone with someone work related, and I just was not in the mood to put the old Mama Kibosh on a fire.

"Hold on a sec," I whisper-hissed to the children, whose dukes were already coming up for a little punching action.

Well, "hold on a sec" is about the most inane thing I could have said, but that's what came to me in the heat of the moment. There was no chance they would pause their sharing scuffle until Mom was off the phone. Kids rarely seem to grasp the art of synchronizing their smack-downs with convenient times for the old referees to get in the ring with them.

"I'm sorry, Brad Pitt, I simply cannot speak with you right now about your intense interest in my co-writing your biography with you. My children, it seems, are poised to commit double homicide momentarily, and I must attend to this matter immediately."

(Well, you know, it might not have been Brad Pitt *exactly* on the phone, but the details are a bit fuzzy.) What I do know is the kids were not sharing their stuff, and it was making them very tense with each other. It was also making me tense with them. I'm sure you can relate.

Preschoolers are famously opposed to sharing their things, especially the under-four set. In fact, only at age four or thereabouts are kiddies now able to grasp concepts like sharing and waiting their turn. The good news is, your four-year-old can now be tutored in the fine art of having joint use of things. The bad news? Her little brother, at age two, doesn't have a clue. (See my book *See How They Run: An Energizing Guide to Keeping Up with Your Turbo Toddler* for more scoop on those cutie-pies called toddlers.)

That is bad news indeed, because no one gets their dukes up over stuff like a couple of siblings. Later, we'll chat more in-depth about the bro-sis, bro-bro, sis-sis rivalry, but for now, let's hone in on sharing and how to finesse your munchkins into doing it.

Why Sharing *Is* Rocket Science for These Guys

"Since we are such selfish creatures, I always tried to keep in mind that it was only *natural* that my child thought that the world revolved around her," says Jen T. "When I started to take Gabbi to a preschool 'Mommy and Me' class, I began to see that every mother had the same difficulties as I did, that my child is not the only child out there that grabs, hits, and will not share that coveted toy."

Why are the little dudes so possessive about their things (or things they think belong to them)? One reason may be that when you're a little kid, nothing really belongs to you. Sure, you may get a yo-yo for your birthday, but when you hit your sister with it, your mom takes it away. It may be your favorite dress, but when you grow out of it, your mother gives it to her best friend's daughter who is littler than you. It may be your special swing at the park, but when you arrive and a big kid is using it, your babysitter tells you to wait your turn. You may start to believe that you have to keep all your important things hidden away to keep them safe from loss.

It's always good to glean a twinkling of insight into pre-schoolers' wee psyches, isn't it? That being said, even though we understand their desire to hoard, we have to encourage them to part with their things for a little while—on a regular basis—in order for them to grow into giving, caring adults. Plus, the constant battles at home can wear a person down to a nub. "When my kids don't share, it can really be a problem for me, especially when I want to get something done," says Alicia. "I feel like I need to be a constant referee sometimes."

23

I'm Not the Center of the Galaxy?

Of course, sharing among siblings is affected by any number of factors, including age span, interests, and gender. Says Cheryl,

> It helps to have a boy and a girl who are a good age span apart (three years and nine months), who generally couldn't care less about each other's toys. We did make an effort especially with Nathanael when he was younger for him to always make sure Adrielle had something to make her "happy"—whether it was "his stuff" or not didn't matter. I think Adrielle just picked up on that from him, and so she generally tries to give Nathanael things to make him happy too.

The "make your sister happy" thing works for me, if only I didn't have two boys who were into each other's stuff. But I can see how the concept works, and it's really quite savvy. If you focus on making each other happy instead of on whose toy is whose, you may even build some character along the way, as in, "Hey, I'm not the center of the galaxy after all, and it feels kinda nice to make someone else feel good for a little while."

Prime the Pump of the Sharing Machine

Here are a few scenarios that may have developed in your home, and a few tips for taking the edge off the daily grind of imparting that biggie life lesson: allowing others to play

24

with one's stuff! But first, a few everyday things you can do to prime the pump of the sharing machine.

Show Off Sharing

Show him it's not a big deal to hand over his stuff once in a while. "Brennan, would you like to have some of my scrapbooking stickers to make a picture with? Mom would be thrilled to share them with you."

Practice Makes Perfect

Get the share-phobic to share toys with *you*. It's often easier for a tot to share with a parent, since she knows you'll be careful and that you'll give the toy back when you're done. This way she can practice sharing "safely."

Save the Speech . . .

For a time when he and his playmate are not brawling over the Spider-Man web blaster. It's not likely he'll drop the toy, look attentively your way, and say, "Oh yes, you're right, Mommy! Sharing is a valuable, character-building experience!" Wait until the heat has died down and teach sharing during times of peace, not war. Obviously, if the two little guys are beating each other, you can step in and blow your whistle. But seriously, parenthood is all in the timing. Don't waste a good lecture on a time when it won't be absorbed.

Mine All the Time

Allow your sweetie to have a few important things that she isn't expected to ever have to loan to her sister, cousin, or playmate. She may be more willing, then, to part with other toys she feels less strongly about. "With my twins we have a 'must share' rule," says Jodi, "*unless* it is a personal stuffed animal or special toy. Generally, if one girl asks nicely and appropriately, the other girl is expected to share."

Grease the Wheels

This age group still desperately needs to be prepared for a change of scenery. Three- to five-year-olds hate to have something sprung on them almost as much as they did when they were toddlers. So whenever possible, lay the groundwork for what is to come, and reap the rewards of a primed child. "I prepare Ashley ahead of time whenever we are going to be with friends or cousins," says Amy. "I just remind her of how important it is to share and be a good friend to others. This usually works very well."

Create a Sharing Story

This one's fun for artistic moms (or dads):

On the first page, show your child refusing to share and his friend frowning. Then show him pondering the options, such as offering a different toy or taking turns. The final entry should be a picture of the children playing together nicely. Read it every day. It will give him cues about how to behave, and soon he'll make the correct choices himself.[1]

The Preschooler/Toddler Tussle

Oooh boy. This one's a classic—the big sib is just learning to get a handle on this issue, but he could very easily be triggered into backsliding into the "mine-field." The problem is that the person doing the triggering is a toddler, the least giving subset of humanity ever. The interesting thing is, the little guy is almost always obsessed with whatever it is the big guy wants or has in his hands at that moment.

Look at This!

Try redirecting the small fry by offering him a toy that won't interest the big fry, or vice versa. As Cheryl said, this is easier when the two kids are a different gender—maybe little sister isn't all that excited over big brother's dump truck, and he's not too thrilled with her Polly Pocket.

Alternatives to Whacking

You can also teach your preschooler some problem-solving skills. Show big brother he can be your helper (he's a firstborn—he wants to run the show anyway) to teach the toddler sib some ground rules. Talk about some scenarios that could crop up, like if the little brother hits the big one when he wants a toy, the big guy could say, "No hitting," instead of whacking back. Or "No grabbing," or "Go play with something else," or better yet, "Here's this fun toy for you to play with." Practice with your tyke in a lighthearted way, gently poking fun at the toddler's ways of doing things, and he'll love being an "insider" and helping Ma and Pa. Be sure to heap praise on him when he follows through.

A Golden-Tidbit Tip

Give your possessive Petunia some options instead of commanding her to dispense with a particular wanted item. "Savannah would like to play with some Polly Pockets. Which ones would you like to let her play with?" This is the golden tip that worked so well with your toddlers—to give a teeny choice that makes your preschooler feel as if she has some control over her life and her stuff when her annoying toddler sister is always eyeballing her goods.

Playing Peacefully

Set up situations in which little Lucy and Lola can play noncompetitively with each other. Take a hotly contested toy out of the picture and instead promote play where the two squabblers can hang out and do an activity alongside each other. Set up parallel playing with Play-Doh (make sure you have plenty to go around for everyone), swinging side by side, finger painting, listening to a story on tape, dancing to music, building a snowman in winter or a sand castle in summer, and so on.

Other options include playing games that require two people, such as lacrosse or Candyland; putting together puzzles in a joint effort; making crafts that require sharing supplies; coloring with one set of crayons or markers; or building a Lego city. "I keep my kids doing something that has lots of pieces, like playing shopping with all the food or something like that," says Alicia. "That way they have lots of things for each of them to play with, and no one fights."

Pay It Forward

Older preschoolers especially respond well to rewards. Instead of pouncing on naughty behavior—grabbing toys, smacking their sib—make a new effort to pay attention to the good stuff. "Maya, I'm going to watch you very closely this week. When you are especially nice to Madison, like when you share your dolls, use words instead of hitting, or

---

"Why Can't You Be More Like Your Cousin Maisie?"

Your niece Maisie was potty trained absurdly early—like eighteen months—and she seems to be developing at a much faster clip than your Moe (who is, at three years and nine months, just now getting to know his way around the loo). But to compare Maisie and Moe is just plain detrimental to your guy. It sparks bewilderment and exasperation, and it won't speed up his development one bit. Comparing how well another child eats, dresses herself, talks, plays, runs, and so on almost always backfires. Your child is not his perfect cousin (who is a bit of a brat, in your private opinion). Instead of pressuring your preschooler to do something he's not yet equipped for, try praising him for the little man he is becoming. "Hey, look how well you used the potty all day today!" "I love your big bear hugs, buddy." "Thanks for sharing that truck with your baby brother."

wait your turn, Mom is going to give you two M&M's, one to eat and one to save. When you've saved five M&M's, Daddy or I will take you to the dollar store for a prize." You'd better believe Maya will be on her best behavior, and she'll love that all her good efforts are going to be compensated. Of course, the child can have the candies taken away when she blows it. Just the threat of not going to the dollar store will probably suffice.[2]

FUN THINGS

Overheard at Preschool, Part 1

Just for smiles, here's a list of too-cute things collected by Jonah and Ezra's fab-oo preschool teachers at Oakdale Christian School. This particular list was from 2002, when Jonah was four and he and his classmates were at their most quotable.

Alex: "I don't have to go potty—I went potty on vacation."

Jennifer: "I went on vacation to NYC and I got to sleep on a bump bed."

Jonah: "I went to North Carolina. It took ten minutes to get to the top part [North Carolina]. Then it took four minutes to get to the bottom part [South Carolina]."

Kate: "Hiccups are like little beeps in your belly."

Myah: "My dad plays with my dollhouse. He plays and I watch."

Sam (to his teacher): "Miss Susan, how many pounds are in your body?"

Caleb: "Mom made Jell-O and it was disastrable!"

Heaven: "First babies come from Jesus, then from a baby shower, then from Mom's tummy."

Samara: "My listening ears have run out of batteries."

Andrew: "I need a cup to protect my penis. I got hit in the penis once, so I NEED a cup!"

Teacher: "What do you know about God?"
Angela: "I pray for him."

Maia: "My nose has been sniffing since this morning."

3

"IF YOU'RE GOING TO KILL EACH OTHER, DO IT IN THE BASEMENT!"

Smoothing the sibling squabbles

"THE FIGHTING THING between Nathanael and Adrielle generally has about nine million factors to it," says mom Cheryl. "How tired are one or both kids? Did one or both kids have an exceptionally bad day (we call that 'fragile')? Are they hungry? Are they bored? Have they been eating too much junk? Is their schedule out of whack, or are they anticipating a visit from friends or grandparents? How crabby and stressed out am I?" Sibling combat or arguments with playmates can wear a parent down to a nub some days. And we've all been there, far more often than we'd like to admit.

"My first daughter is a very strong-willed little individual," says Jen T. "She gives back what she receives from those surrounding her, and she also originates the [fight] very often. I find that my yelling only creates more chaos in this situation." Jen usually separates Gabbi from her opponents (playmates, in this case, since Gabbi's sib is a baby), and they have a serious chat about how to treat others.

With twin three-year-olds, Jodi faces this crisis often during her day. "I would love to know the 'answer' to getting my kids not to argue about everything," she says. "We have 'Kindness Rules' written on the refrigerator: no taking toys, no hitting, pushing, fighting, or kicking, and they must share with one another and use kind words. If these rules are broken, they are sent to time-out and then must ask the other sibling for forgiveness."

Both moms have sound techniques in dealing with the frequent spats that erupt with their preschoolers. I have used the time-out, put-the-monkeys-in-separate-cages approach myself many times. But recently I've come upon an even better way to deal with fractious infighting between my darling sons. It is a philosophy that seems all at once radically new and classically wise. Since I've been employing this procedure with my angels, I've seen the kind of results I love to see. Let's call the plan . . .

Lorilee's Lightbulb Moment

"My mother's favorite phrase when my brother and I were fighting was 'If you're going to kill each other, go do it in the basement,'" says Cheryl. It may sound a wee bit harsh, but according to experts, Cheryl's mom was on to

34

something brilliant. If we as parents take ourselves out of the ring, the pugnacious little pugs will calm down presto. Turns out they didn't want to kill each other after all; they just wanted some face time with Ma and Pa.

Kevin Leman prescribes a similar solution to basic brawling. He tells parents to give their kids license to go at it, just not two feet away from where mom is on the phone or where dad is reading a magazine on the couch. "In most cases," he says, "when you give children permission to fight, they won't. They merely stand and look at each other. . . . Their fighting, for the most part, was designed to get the parents needlessly involved in their hassles."[1] (Aha!) "The sooner parents learn to stay out of their child's hassles the sooner they will teach their children greater responsibility and accountability."[2]

Anthony E. Wolf, the author of *Mom, Jason's Breathing on Me!* concurs: "The moment an adult becomes part of the equation, any rational, interested-in-working-on-resolutions part of the child disappears, leaving in its stead the mindless, raving version whose only interest is getting all of mom or dad."[3]

Mindless and raving sounds about right, doesn't it? So we have to figure out how to get our mommy-selves out of the equation, which is easier than it sounds. Cheryl's mom was obviously a cool, jaded *madre* who had seen it all and knew what her kids were after—and it wasn't each other's blood. I admit, it's hard for me to just stand by, cool as a cucumber, when Jonah is hurting Ezra's feelings, or Ezra is provoking Jonah beyond what he can bear. But I find the more I practice "disengaging" from their tussles, the more even-keeled things around the Craker casa have been.

Needed: Family Referee with Nerves of Steel

Don't take sides. Unless they are about to really, truly hurt each other, just be as neutral as possible. Think, "I am Switzerland. I am Switzerland. I am Switzerland." Have some Swiss chocolate if it helps your frame of mind (which it will).

"Mom! Jake poked me in the back with his Star Wars guy!" your son Josh complains. You bristle because you saw that very thing happen out of the corner of your eye, and you are fed up with Jake bugging his brother. But you resist the urge to intervene on Josh's side, because intervention means the jig is up.

"Josh, that sounds annoying," you say in a calm, unruffled tone of voice, immediately returning to that magazine you were reading.

Josh, shocked by your patent disinterest in his plight, will dial it up a notch.

"Mom! I said Jake poked me, hard! It *hoyts*! It *hoyts*!"

"Josh, Mom'll kiss it better, OK, sweets?" (You know it hurts, a little, but are quite sure it won't even bruise the next day. No blood, no foul.)

Meanwhile, Jake is standing there, completely thrown off his game and unsure how to proceed. He's just where you want him. Josh is still trying to claim his injury. One more try: "Jake bwoke a *wule*! Mommy! He bwoke a *wule* 'bout no hoyting me!"

At this point, you may think you'll never finish that article until you clamp down on the offender and the offended one. But hang in there, says Wolf, and continue trying to keep out of it. "The technique," he writes, "can be boiled down to saying seven simple words: 'I don't want to hear about it.'"[4]

So you give it a whirl: "I don't want to hear about it right now, Josh. You two can work it out." Sounds cold, doesn't it? But remember, Mom, beneath your chilly exterior beats the heart of a parent who wants her kid to learn how to cope when someone is bugging him. When you let your precious child fight his own battles, you give him life-shaping gifts. He learns how hard to shove and when to retreat. Basically, the sibling smack-down is a golden opportunity for your children to compromise and just plain get along better with everyone they encounter. Cling to this thought when you want to waffle and cave in.

Of course, this may not be the end of the matter. Depending on how mulish your tyke is, he may keep trying for some attention from you. Or he may come to the realization that it is between him and his brother, and you aren't about to get embroiled in their petty little scuffles after all.

Pieces of Mommy Are Not Up for Grabs

Your kids basically want a piece of you, Mom, and when you jump in every time they are busting each other's chops, you are doing them a big disservice. You're not going to be out there in the big, bad world with them every time they get into an argument with someone. When you're not there to scold or ask who started it, guess what? The little ankle biters will be forced to forge peace on their own.

And hopefully, next time they want to start an altercation, they'll think twice about the payoff. "Mom won't take the bait, so why even bother?" Stand firm and remember how important it is for your little ones to work out problems on their own. You have only so many pieces of yourself to part with. Don't give them away so easily.

FUN THINGS

Heck Yeah, I Want a Medal (and a Chest to Pin It On)! Part 1

I want a medal . . .

For thirty hours of mind-boggling labor (that was four years ago, but one never forgets such things) while the man whose progeny came forth out of my body patted my hand and asked if I was "OK."

For all the boogers I have removed from my child's nose with my bare hands.

For all the used tissues handed to me on the blind assumption I wanted to hold them.

For taking my kids to the doctor for their immunizations, especially that traumatic, never-to-be-forgotten visit for the two-month shots.

For not crashing the minivan all those times my preschooler let out a whoop about something, causing me to think there was a flying television set or an elephant crossing the road.

For, in the midst of a four-day family flu, hauling my weary bones, swimming head, and running nose off the couch and to the pharmacy to fill the other family members' prescriptions.

For letting them out of my sight, ever, after hearing some scary news report on TV.

For, instead of watching the chick flick DVD I'd been dying to see ever since it came out in theaters (five months before), cleaning up toddler puke and then being too tired to do anything but go to bed.

For one word: Barney!

4

BEYOND CEREAL, GRILLED CHEESE, AND PB&J

Getting your finicky eater to expand his menu

"Are You Calling the Police?"

Three-year-old Bennett refused to eat the eggs he had requested for breakfast, but because mom Alanna had already prepared them, she insisted he eat them. In fact, little Ben was not allowed to leave the table until he had downed his fluffy yellow breakfast. "After a half hour of listening to Ben fuss, I decided to call my husband, Rick, at work about something completely unrelated to eating. Ben, still at the table grumbling about his eggs, got very fidgety and wide eyed. 'Are you calling the police?' he asked nervously. Ben gobbled down his breakfast before Rick and I were even finished talking!"

Wouldn't it be nice sometimes to involve the men in blue in our daily altercations over food? As it is, moms are the food cops anyway. Preschoolers are truly America's Most Wanted picky eaters, and that issue can drive a mom batty. What's worse is that our preschoolers were decent eaters in the past, and then one day they woke up and realized, *Hey, I'm three, and I'm only supposed to like five foods.* Then the fun starts. Jen T. can attest.

> I put *so much* effort into Gabbi's diet when she first started eating. I made all of Gabbi's food from scratch for her first year and a half. She would eat anything: cabbage, spinach, avocado, whole grain foods, and so on. Now it's a totally different story. Gabbi is three-and-a-half years old, and she will not touch most things she used to love. We compromise on certain foods like having instant brown sugar oatmeal instead of homemade oatmeal, but she is a typical kid; Gabbi would live on candy and marshmallows if she could.

Picky: Discriminating, Fastidious, Choosy . . .

Does your demi-diner sniff every morsel of food she eats, asking, "Is chicken supposed to smell like this?" Have you cut enough crusts off PB&J sandwiches to cover the Yellow Brick Road? Will you run down the street screaming if your four-year-old asks for his hamburger with no bun, no ketchup, no cheese, no lettuce, definitely no pickles, and no meat (leaving you with no choice but to smear a glop of mayo on his plate in the hopes he'll lick it and get some fat calories)?

Sounds like you've got a persnickety little eater on your hands. (Pretty much nine out of ten preschoolers are picky critters.) What makes a mom more unhinged than the effort of coaxing sustenance into the mouth of her precious, darling progeny? Not much. And as we know by now, the list of foods these guys and girls actually profess to like is short—and sweet: anything sugarcoated is de rigueur. So din-din becomes a battleground and food a source of frustration. "Grace's staples are hot dogs, Mac-n-Cheese, and PB&J," says Christy. "If I get some fruit in there during the day, I consider it a success."

It's hard for a grown-up to wrap her mind around a tyke's resistance to food. We love food, right? We can't wait to try new restaurants or indulge in old favorites like Mom's barbeque meatloaf and mashed spuds. Food is essential to our culture. We use it to celebrate our triumphs and console ourselves in time of loss. Not only is eating a key element of our society, but what we eat is tied to the culture to which we belong.

Burdock Root, Anyone?

We as North Americans think that our kiddies won't like "exotic" foods—anything other than hot dogs, grilled cheese, Cheerios, and chicken fingers—so we never offer them any in the first place. Even though your three-year-old ain't touching a pita stuffed with olives, feta cheese, and baba ghanoush, some kid the same exact age and gender across the world in, say, Jordan, gobbles up the stuff.

43

A 1998 article in the *Wall Street Journal* underscored this concept that our children's food likes and dislikes are hugely culture bound. The best-selling flavor of Gerber-brand baby food in Japan at that time was (drumroll please) . . . rice with chopped burdock root and sardines ground up in white radish sauce. (I don't even know what a burdock root is!) We'd no sooner get our junior family members to wolf down sardines than we'd get them to sleep in a pitch-dark room with no night-lights.[1]

Then again, sometimes I think it's all in the presentation. Kids can be taught to enjoy "exotic" foods if that's what we expect from them and that's what we serve them from day one. "Since my husband comes from Nigeria, I've learned to cook several dishes from his culture, as well as the variety you can find in America with our melting pot of cultures and tastes," says Kim. "So my girls have grown up eating rice, spicy meats, and everything else 'American.'"

One more illustration. I grew up in a Russian Mennonite family, and we ate the dense, dark, rich, black Russian rye bread our grandparents brought over from the mother country. To this day, a slice of Wonder Bread strikes me as namby-pamby.

All of that to say there's a whole world of culinary adventures out there, just waiting to be sampled one nibble at a time. As moms, our notions about what foods kids will like are arbitrary. And just because our kids won't eat something out of their comfort zone—which we created for them, by the way—doesn't mean it's not incredibly appealing, nutritious, and edible to millions of children out there.

So we're basically back to square one (except for the rather eye-opening visual of Japanese babies whose faces are smeared in white radish sauce): our fastidious feeders still won't partake of (fill in the blank), no matter what.

When finicky Freddy turns up his nose at your secret chicken recipe, it makes you want to pull out your hair. After all, rejecting food is an unimaginable luxury for most of the world's children! Yet here sits Fred, lip out, scowling, arms crossed, refusing to let one delicious morsel down the hatch.

That little scenario pushes my buttons; how about you? But getting mad only makes things worse, and some experts say pushing too hard might make Fred's eating problems worse.

So what *can* we do to help our tiny tots eat their tater tots and everything else on the menu? I'm glad you asked.

What's a Mom to Do?

The bad news is, some kids are not going to be great eaters—no way, no how. Extreme cases aside, however, the world's choosiest eaters can be cajoled into broadening their pea-sized palates. It just takes a measure of insight into their brains, a scoop of knowledge about their physiology, a pinch of patience, and lots and lots of cheese. But first, a few general notes about pint-sized epicures (or anti-epicures, as it were) and our common worries about their diet.

A Little Biology Lesson

First, keep in mind that things just taste different to kids. "Their taste buds are generally more sensitive and may be overwhelmed by the spiciness of a dish that their parents would consider intolerably bland. Young children especially avoid bitter tastes, such as those found in dark green vegetables."[2] Aha! So the child is not just being pugnacious when she refuses her spinach!

Don't Panic—Yet

What do you mean, don't panic? That's easy for you to say, Miss Lorilee, because your child is not on a world-record–setting food jag that includes about four items!

Well, er, I guess it is kind of easy for me to say that, but the truth is, your pediatrician will back me up here. If Mr. PB&J won't diversify his proteins in any way, shape, or form, it's still OK as long as he's healthy and not losing weight. Throw in a chewable vitamin, and you've most likely got your bases covered. But it's still easy to worry, isn't it? "What I've learned is not a trick or a tip, but sound advice from our doctor: do not obsess about what she eats," says SuperMomNot, a member of Parent Soup, a popular parenting website. "OK, so I still obsess about it somewhat, especially last year when she was losing weight, but I just don't let her know I am concerned about it. What I have done is put her on a good multivitamin with iron, offered her healthy choices to eat, and left her alone. I keep yogurt, fruit, cheese cubes, and fresh veggies ready to eat in the refrigerator for her to pull out whenever she wants."

Here's the good news: this too shall pass. If you don't have a big fat cow about it, persnickety Pete will probably grow bored with his blah diet within a few weeks. Sometimes the best thing to do is let the little person leave the table after a reasonable amount of time, like Sharon does with her choosy child, Carissa. "We don't really want to make food a battleground, so Carissa just leaves hungry rather than having to sit by the table for an hour after everyone else has left," Sharon says. "She has energy. Her hair shines. She can complete sentences most of the time, so I figure she is getting enough to exist on for now." Of course, the trick here is to stand firm and not cave in with a snack later. The child will survive until breakfast, I promise.

"You'd Better Eat That Lima Bean Soufflé!"

Ah yes, the ever-popular force-feeding method, a parenting technique used since the dawn of time. (Of course, in many parts of the world, children eat whatever they can get their hands on, which makes us North American moms feel worse about our own kids' choosiness!) We are probably less black-and-white about making our children clean their plates than our moms were, but variations on forcing the issue still exist. "Getting Grace to eat dinner is a struggle," says Christy. "We usually use the 'Eat this many pieces, and if you don't finish, no dessert,' or 'If you're hungry later, this [food] is it,' and we save it."

Why, oh why, is this such a familiar scenario? At our house, last night's squash was buttered and brown-sugared and as gussied up as any orange-hued puree could be. And it was delicious, if I do say so myself (and loaded with vitamin A). But Ezra would not touch it with a ten-foot pole. We talked it up (enthusiasm!). We ate ours with gusto (role modeling!). Even the big brother ate his with little commentary (peer pressure!). But the four-year-old would not budge, until we "budged" him by insisting he have two spoonfuls before leaving the table.

Why is the dinner table such a battleground sometimes? Preschoolers have known since they were toddlers that eating, like toilet training, is an effective way to gain control of a situation, to throw their weight around a little bit. To a four-year-old, spurning what his mom is trying to sweet-talk into his mouth may be much more important than the taste of the food in question.[3] Keep in mind that little Howie is most likely trying to engage you in a power struggle, so

Will Force-Feeding Lead to Eating Disorders?

"My husband gets concerned when our three-year-old refuses to eat her food," says Kim of her daughter Elana. "I figure she'll eat what she needs to eat. He, on the other hand, has on occasion forced her to eat. This worries me, as I've heard that it can cause eating disorders in the future. Anyway, my policy is that she needs to eat her meals—no snacks until she does." Our generation of mothers is convinced an eating disorder is right around the corner if we make one false move at the dinner table, but c'mon, let's think about this a minute. Did we not grow up hearing the "eat your beets or no dessert" speech? Look how we turned out! Some of us even like beets. Insisting that your fastidious Franny choke down two spoonfuls of spinach is hardly going to cause an eating disorder, though you may influence her body image in other ways (see chap. 13).

your best tactic here may be to just step out of the ring. He won't starve, and he'll know better than to turn up his nose at perfectly good lima bean soufflé next time you serve it.

If You Eat Your Okra, You Can Drive the SUV Up and Down the Driveway

I have a feeling this resorting-to-bribery business has been around since the knuckle-dragging cavemen days ("Ug, you eat dat slab meat and you get velociraptor ride later"). But this will backfire big-time. Experts say disproportionate rewards for eating a particular food tend to make children like that food even less. Think about that next time you feel the urge to dangle sugary treats or movies or TV or later bedtime as enticements for healthy eating. "My basic premise is that when a child doesn't want to eat, bribing and rewarding aren't going to work," says Kevin Leman in his book *Making Children Mind without Losing Yours*. So what do you do instead of bribing and cajoling to get a food-resistant child to eat? "Hold him accountable for his choice. Remove the food from the plate, dump it in the garbage (or save it in the fridge), and excuse the children from the table. This works with ten-year-olds as well as three-year-olds." Buzz Jr. will eat a gi-normous breakfast, says Dr. Leman, and "that missed meal will do much to teach your child what reality is all about."[4]

Would You Like Fries or Cole Slaw with That?

"At home our kids are required to eat what's on the table," says Alanna. "I'm not running a restaurant, so there's no choice as to what we're having!" Sometimes, though, it's tempting to do the short-order cook routine, isn't it? My preschool panel got quite opinionated about this topic:

Johana: I remind my kids that they will not get anything else to eat if they don't eat what's on the table. And if what we have prepared is tough for little ones to eat, then they (not me) can fix themselves a PB&J.

Cheryl: Finicky eating is a pet peeve of mine. I cook a lot, and I cook from scratch. I make a lot of exotic things and try new recipes regularly. And if I do that, they are going to eat it. If they whine, "I don't like that," especially if they haven't tried it, my usual reply is, "I don't care. It's what we're having for dinner, and you are going to eat it." They always have to try a food and eat at least three bites of it. And I'm proud to say my kids eat really well now and have very broad palates.

Sharon: If we ate the same three meals over and over again, we would be fine. But I need variety and really want my kids to have more expanded taste buds than just for spaghetti and hot dogs. Maybe I shouldn't be worrying so much about that now, but I had a friend in grade school who was catered to as a child and was very finicky, and she still is to this day, so I do not do the short-order cook thing. We ask for one bite to find out if Carissa truly does not like it. With the veggies she has to eat some bites before departing.

Remember Alanna saying she wasn't running a restaurant? Neither are you, girlfriend! Short-order cooking for your kids will make you resentful and will spoil them rotten, like Sharon's friend who was so coddled as a child that she's now a fussy grown-up (is there anything worse?). If you have prepared something reasonably family friendly—that is, not sautéed escargot with leek infusion—but Junior can't wrap his appetite around it, then you have two options. First, you could insist that he try two or three bites. Or try the eat-as-many-bites-as-your-age routine, which appeals to a kid's logic. "That's how my mom got me to eat peas, even if it was only six of them!" says Alanna. "Now I take generous helpings of peas, so I think there is *some* hope concerning Max and Bennett's 'un-favorites'!"

On rare occasions—and only if you've whipped up some dish with a universally low popularity rating—option two is to have your munchkin fix himself a PB&J. Obviously, a five-year-old can accomplish this with less mess than a three-year-old, but it's a good notion to start your kids out young with helping themselves. After all, Mommy won't be accompanying Howie III to Yale so she can spread peanut butter on his toast.

Ten Tips for Getting Your Preschooler to Eat Better Stuff

Finito on the Fluids

Does your child slosh when you tickle her? That may be your first clue that the child is gulping down too much milk, juice, or pop. And if her tummy is full of those high-calorie or high-fat liquids, well, there's simply no room for carrots, chicken, and mashed potatoes. Tons of kids drink too many liquids that blunt their appetites for solid foods. I learned this fact, oddly enough, while visiting a certain

German aunt who boasts a rather forceful personality. Let me call her Tante Hilda, just to disguise her identity. (I have an assortment of German aunts with forceful personalities.) We were enjoying our second meal with Tante Hilda when one of my children asked for some milk. It was then that I noticed the kids' cups were empty. Camera panned to the Hildanator, who calmly said, "Nein, no milche fur dein Kinder. At lunch dey got filled up on milche und dey didn't eat der meat. After dey eat der food—den vee get dem zum milche!" Wide eyed—and parched—the boys shoveled in their sauerbraten without delay.

My point here is that Tante Hilda was right. Nutritional science bears this out too. So limit juice to one glass mid-morning and one glass mid-afternoon, and keep milk to about two glasses a day. Offer unlimited water, and add ice flavored with juice for a while if it sweetens the deal. If Normie claims to be thirsty but balks at drinking water, you're on to him: he just wants something sweet, and he's not that arid after all. Amy clipped little Ashley's juice habit, and it not only boosted her appetite but also resulted in a cool fringe benefit. "Ashley has now reported that she is a 'water drinker' and has given up juice," Amy says. Tante Hilda would say "wunderbar" to that!

"Wednesday: Play with Your Food"

This quote by Miss Morticia from *The Addams Family* was right on the money: when we allow our little ones to be playful with their food, we dial up the fun factor and entice them to nosh on healthy food. This doesn't mean playing "stick the noodle to the wall," but it does mean rolling fajitas or topping personal pizzas, tacos, pitas, and wrapped sandwiches. It means broccoli trees, Bob-the-Tomato casserole, and "bugs" made out of apple slices with raisin eyes. It means a drop of red food coloring in a container of ranch dressing becomes pink "princess dip," and spaghetti squash becomes "orange worms." (For St. Patrick's Day, I added green food coloring to a tuna noodle dish, and the kids got a big bang out of it—they even ate every bite. Jo Jo and Ez usually have words when I make this concoction, but this time they ate it because it was *green*.) Writer Nancy Kennedy talks about her pal's attempts to add some sizzle to dinner:

> Take it from my friend Patty, there's nothing too far fetched when it comes to getting kids to eat. Afraid she'd be labeled a failure as a mother because her kids wouldn't eat broccoli or peas, one night she told them: "Kids, after you went to sleep last night I found a jar of fairy dust—and here it is!" She held up a jar of finely ground parmesan cheese. "This does something wonderful. It makes anything you eat taste delicious."
>
> At dinner that evening she let the kids sprinkle fairy dust all over their lasagna (which was full of zucchini and other green things), saying, "Not only will this taste wonderful, but it will make you stronger and taller! You'll be able to lift heavy toys and put them away, and you'll be able to reach a little higher than before so you can get a drink of water without calling for me or Daddy."
>
> Patty's ploy actually worked—until her daughter caught her refilling the fairy jar with store-bought parmesan. Now she's back to sneaking green stuff into gingerbread.

The moral of this story? Don't get caught, but do get creative with ways to add a little snap, crackle, and pop to your family foodstuffs. Lure veggie-phobics with custom-colored dip or salad dressing so they can plunge peapods to their heart's content. Tempt finicky fruit eaters with a little bowl—just for them—filled with yogurt, applesauce, or sweet cream cheese. Like Patty, powder whatever you're having with a sprinkle of parmesan cheese or, if it's fruity, a dusting of cake-decorating sprinkles. Call it "fairy dust" or "the sand between a monster's toes"—whatever you think will fly with your kids.

Get Saucy

There's nothing like a dousing of cheese sauce to make a hill of cooked brussels sprouts look and taste more appetizing. Or how about a yummy alfredo sauce, or even ketchup? I have a theory that during the choosy preschool years, parents can try whatever works to get their little food snobs to open up their mouths. Yes, that includes ketchup, which is actually good for you, especially when not used exclusively on fries. But when those preschool years are over, I think they will let go of putting ketchup on everything just as easily as they let go of thumb sucking when they were toddlers. Let the tyke squirt his own condiment too for good measure. This is, after all, the "me do it myself" era.

Liquefy It

"Sometimes I get sneaky and I will make Gabbi a fruit shake made out of mangos, yogurt, wheat germ, a little honey, and various other things," says Jen T. "Then I know that she has gotten some good vitamins in her diet." I've known one mom who had great success with this trick, incorporating all her child's leftovers (including tuna!) in a blender with ice cream and fruit. Sounds gross, but when you think about it, the plan makes sense: kids love milk shakes or smoothies, and many of them adore any kind of experimentation too. So get out your blender and see what happens when you mix bananas, yogurt, a little ice cream, and some apple juice. Throw in carrot juice (it's through-the-roof in vitamin A), brain-boosting flax, and whatever nutrient-rich foods you think might be successfully snuck in there, and watch in smug satisfaction as picky Missy gulps it down.

Make Mine Delicious

This nifty notion comes from Parent Soup member Jennie0264:

One day I happened to say to my four-year-old daughter that since she wasn't going to eat the "good stuff" on her plate, I was going to give it to her little sister, who had downed her own in seconds flat. It was then that she said, "Maybe I'll try it after all." She took a bite and said, "This is delicious!" I told her, "I'd never put anything on your plate that wasn't delicious." That is now a motto around here at dinnertime, and I make her repeat it whenever she success-fully tries something new. "You'd never put anything on my plate that wasn't delicious." She says this giggling as she polishes her plate clean. It's been a long five months, but I think she's finally come out of the stage—for now, anyway. My only difficulty is sifting through all those recipes to make sure I only make the "delicious" ones.[5]

Ask for Audience Participation

When Ezra balks at going to preschool, I ask him to help me make his lunch or to pick out a snack. It seems like such a small thing, but getting him involved in the process and giving him some say over what he's eating makes all the difference. Need more proof? One time Ez gobbled down a plateful of paella after he had served as my sous-chef and squeezed the sausage out of the casings into the pan. It was a mild, simplified paella (i.e., no mussels or otherwise exotic sea creatures with bulbous eyeballs or visible bowels), but he had no qualms about scarfing down *fish stew*, which strikes me as remarkable.

So encompass your tots in the cooking process whenever you can, and give them a personal stake, if you will, in their food. Even your three-year-old should be able to pour something from a measuring cup into a bowl or wash vegetables or push buttons on the microwave. New or odd edibles are a lot less sinister to little Harry when he's become comfortable with them away from the battleground—I mean, table. Along the same lines, have your variety-resistant small person help plan menus and with the shopping. One mom has had success with a "menu": "Write down the menu and put it on the calendar. That way he can see that he is going to have grilled cheese, oranges, and carrots for lunch. Having a menu also makes it official—if you have it on the menu, there won't be any whining. Even if your child is pre-reading, you can say, 'The menu says we are having this for lunch today. I am really sorry that you want something else. Maybe you could choose it for our menu next week.'" Blame it on the menu—I love it!

Be Sly

Oh yeah, motherhood can be one underhanded operation sometimes. When you're chopping the broccoli so finely it's hardly visible to the naked eye, you're being as furtive as an undercover agent on a top-secret mission. And your mission—should you choose to accept it—is to sneak some healthy stuff into foods your preschooler actually likes. This means tucking a few extra veggies in lasagna, spaghetti sauce, soup, chili, and casseroles. Or you could throw in grated carrots or zucchini in quick breads, cakes (carrot cake was invented by the mother of a picky eater!), or even meatballs or meatloaf.

Finesse with Freezer Foods

For some strange reason known only to four-year-olds and their ilk, young children will often warm up faster to a food that comes out of the freezer than the oven—especially if it's summer. Hey, it worked incredibly well for Kim and her two tots, Elana and Oliana. "I had heard that frozen veggies are great teethers, so I tried peas when they were getting some teeth in and now they beg for them when I open the freezer!" she says. "A friend of mine had even brought frozen lima beans to the park for her daughter. My daughter had some and now she likes those too." Lima beans are pretty impressive, but get this: "My girls also have another strange passion—raw onions. When I was cooking one day, one of my daughters asked me what the minced onions were and begged for some. So, thinking by giving her a taste she'd never ask for them again, I gave her some. Now I can hardly get them in the pot before she's eaten half of them. At times like those, dealing with onion breath is the real challenge!"

But seriously, folks, you can freeze slices of mango, peaches, and pineapple or a whole banana on a popsicle stick. Or try partially thawing some cherries, strawberries, peas, or even lima beans and serving them in a bowl with a sprinkle of sugar or salt. The key is keeping the food at

Good Carbs and Fats

In this age of childhood obesity, we hear tons of info on limiting carbohydrates and fats in our kids' diets. But the key is to fuel their energy with good fats and carbs and avoid the junky ones. Smart choices? Strawberries, peaches, oranges, and blueberries are nice and sweet and still provide fantastic vitality for your revved-up tykes. Sweet potatoes, veggies, whole-grain breads and pastas, yogurt, and oatmeal are also good carbs for kids. Watch out for sugar-loaded, processed foods, which cause your child's blood-sugar levels to pinnacle and then quickly plunge. Is there such a thing as a good fat (we may ask)? Actually, yes, both for your sweetie and for you, especially in the form of omega-3 fats found in salmon, sea bass, freshwater trout, avocados, eggs, and peanut butter. These fab fats actually build smarter brains in growing bodies.

glacial temperatures; then watch your anti-veggie guy or girl chill out and pop a few peas!

Wait for a Rumbly in His Tumbly

It's an hour after preschool, and at least another before dinner. The "I'm sooo hungry" comments are escalating, and there's only one thing to do: hand over a bag of carrots. Then watch your child eat the whole thing. It seems so obvious, but a preschooler will be much more open to imbibing healthy foods (fruits and veggies especially) when he's hungry than when he's got a tummy full of other foods. Wait until your little one is complaining of being famished, then produce a platter of dippable veggies and her favorite dipping sauce. Watch amazed as she nibbles contentedly on carrots and cauliflower.

If at First You Don't Succeed . . .

Try, try again. "Months after putting a dish on the table that Madison doesn't like, I'll revisit that meal again," says Johana. "Usually she will eat it up the second try." Expect your picky Missy to turn up her nose at new foods the first few times she encounters them. But don't give up on getting her to eat salmon. Studies show that children sometimes accept a food they originally rejected after they've been exposed to it as many as ten to fifteen times.[6] So keep offering her favorite dishes along with the "un-yummy" ones, and in time, she may eat that grilled salmon—and like it too!

59

Heck Yeah, I Want a Medal (and a Chest to Pin It On)! Part 2

I want a medal . . .

For every second on the phone with poison control.

For peeling grapes, removing the microscopic fibers of herb from the ranch dressing, and when we were at the park and sans peeler, methodically biting off and spitting out all the skin on the apple.

For digging through the sock pile (known as the quagmire) and coming up with semi-matching boy's hosiery every single day.

For coming up with responses to statements from planet Random Thoughts, such as, "Mom! I can't find my eyebrows!"

For handling sibling scuffles starting with the words, "Mom! Jonah called me a swear!"

For "hurrying" a toddler and then a preschooler umpteen times, when really I would have had as much success rushing our pet snail, Judy, to eat her lettuce. Or shoving a mule down the road.

For walking through the hallways at school after learning that my child, during preschool prayer circle, asked for prayer—and twenty four-year-olds went home and told their parents—that his mommy's breasts would feel better because they were sore.

For one word: backwash!

5

MOMMY'S GOING TO THE MAT!

Picking your battles

"NO PANTS! I want to wear my pajamas!" My three-year-old was filled with righteous indignation over my suggestion that it was time to get on a shirt and pants for preschool. His arms were folded over his chest, and his lip jutted out in defiance. Irritated and about to run late, I dug in my heels. "Ez, you have to wear clothes to school!"

"I *am* wearing clothes!" The child even stomped his foot at that statement. But he did have a point. It wasn't like he wanted to go flouncing off to school in his birthday suit, although that scenario was certainly possible. *Let's cross that bridge when we come to it,* I figured, hoping fervently we wouldn't.

Faced with this flannel-clad bundle of opposition and with about five minutes to put out this fire—or fuel it—I made a choice to let this one go.

"Ez, you may not talk to me like that, but you may wear your Thomas the Tank Engine jammies *if* you ask nicely." Stunned that he could actually be allowed to do so, Ezra acquiesced. He unfolded his arms, un-pouted his lower lip, and then asked nicely if he could please wear his pajamas to school.

The thought flitted through my mind that my mother never, under any circumstances, would have allowed her little child to attend school or any other public function wearing pajamas. She would have as soon burned her bra in a front-yard bonfire and declared herself a patriot of the women's liberation movement.

But I, semi-liberated and wearing a bra, picked a battle in that moment. Or rather, I picked "no" on fighting that particular battle. Why? Well, it's preschool, not the SATs. You know, finger painting and cookie baking, an unstructured, winsome place where whimsy and wonder abound. I knew he would be sufficiently warm and decently clothed, and also that his whimsical teachers wouldn't blink an eye over Ezra's one-man pajama day. (Indeed, Miss Susan and Miss Catharine celebrated his entrance with great fanfare and made a big fuss over how silly and funny and wonderful Ezra was to wear his pajamas to school!)

Motherhood is crammed with opportunities to pick a battle or to step out of the ring. I could have forcibly stripped Ezra of his pajamas and then wrestled him into some school clothes. Or maybe I could have threatened him with consequences. The thing is, I knew it would be a huge ordeal to "force" him to do what he so clearly didn't want to do. Was it easier to let him attend class wearing his jammies? Absolutely.

This child has a will so steely it boggles my mind. We could be in the ring all day long at times, duking it out over some disagreement or other. But if I turn every misdemeanor into a felony, I'll lose my maternal authority and probably my mind. Shaping and guiding a preschooler's moral character will be a long, hard slog, so I've learned to save my energy for the lessons he really has to learn.

This age is highly combative too. The amount of arguing and disobeying peaks between four and five, say experts. These guys are bent on getting what they want, and now they have a new way to go after it: with language. By now, most tykes have about eight thousand words in their vocabularies.[1]

We would rather argue the finer points of appropriate wardrobe with a chatty, erudite little man than cope with an incoherent, frustrated toddler, but it still can be wearing to go head-to-head twenty times a day with someone we love.

So we pick our battles to save energy, preserve peace, and give our kids some options over things that are really not that important in the grand scheme of things. What, then, are the important things, the matters for which we moms would go to the mat, time after time, until we've won?

Health and safety issues are nonnegotiable—duh! But what other conflicts are worth choosing, and which petty clashes should be deemed unworthy of our motherly grit, toughness, and resolve?

"Could You Please Wear Something Else?"

Listen to my preschool panel talk about their battles of choice.

Sharon: Carissa has very distinct tastes in clothes (already!). She will want to wear the same pants, shirt, or whatever every day until I come up with a new alternative. Dirty, clean, torn, tie-dyed with rhinestones! We have had many frustrating mornings kneeling next to her dresser pulling out other options. Too tight, too loose, she says. But mostly Carissa scrunches up her face and shakes her head. I really have to let this go, because I see all these "cute" outfits on her preschool friends and I am lucky to get her into two separates that barely match. It doesn't matter, it doesn't matter, I tell myself. What's important is what is on the inside. *She is a great kid, Sharon*, I tell myself. It doesn't matter what she is wearing. Sometimes this self-talk works, but I am hoping this is just a phase.

Amy: Our major battle with Ashley right now is to stop her from being so bossy. Instead of saying, "I want more noodles now!" we have been working on phrasing it, "Mommy, could I have more noodles, please?" We currently started putting pennies in a sundae dish when she uses her manners. It seems to be helping, temporarily anyway.

Kim: I suppose it depends on my mood—some days I have more patience, others not so much. But I'm trying to be better about when I apply discipline—and what for. Hitting a sibling or talking back to Mom or Dad are definite no-no's. Respect of adults in my husband's culture (Nigerian) is of the utmost importance, so I try to emphasize that. When my kids go to school I want them to respect their teacher and even their friends' parents. It's definitely hard in our day and age, but I figure the earlier I start the better.

Cheryl: Generally I pick battles that involve their general well-being or will benefit them (and me!) over the long term. Eating good food (and not just junk). Hanging up their own coats and putting their boots away. Cleaning up their own messes—I'll pitch in, but not without their help! Basically, I don't want to be the slave mom who does everything forever and resents it—my kids do need to know some basic life skills here! And if it's something that will endanger them physically (like riding a bike without a helmet), spiritually, or mentally (crummy TV), I definitely fight it.

Don't Freak Out over the Small Stuff

Let's say you're working on kindness, reminding your preschooler throughout the day to talk nicely to her brother, or you, or Mrs. Pickles, your corpulent neighbor. Then at dinner she wipes her mouth on her sleeve, and you are tempted to freak (you picture her at her prom, dabbing her pomodoro-sauced mouth on her date's tuxedo). But you hold back, because she's made some real progress in the kindness department (she hasn't told Mrs. Pickles lately that she's as fat as Willa Mae, the pig from the petting zoo), and blowing up over a manners issue will only detract from the lessons learned that day. Of course, the next day, if you've only gotten after her once for calling her brother a dork face, you may feel you have some "currency" left to spend on etiquette issues. The point is, one big thing at a time. Weigh the hot-button issues du jour and decide if what happens next is worth a crackdown from Ma.

Do Use Four Little Words

"Do you want to . . . ?"

Three- to five-year-olds are convinced that every single thing that happens is connected to what they think, say, or do. As a group, preschoolers are only slightly less narcissistic than toddlers. The upshot? Each decision is hugely important to your child, plus her choices are broadening as she gets older. Little Ava's gamut of choice now includes food, clothes, activities (the park or the library?), entertainment (*Dora* or *Jo Jo's Circus?*), and how to spend some family time (the beach or riding bikes?). She will also want to decide when to go to bed, whether to brush her hair, and when to turn off the TV.

Saving Face with a Win-Win Scenario

This, my friends, is a tool so valuable it makes me shudder to think of going through parenthood without it! Here's how it works: you're in the trenches with Ava, who is fighting you tooth and nail about taking a bath. Her fingernails are grubby, her left ear could grow a potato plant behind it, and her whole persona is wafting with the miasma of eau de wet dog. She needs a good dunking for sure. But not surprisingly, Ava would rather play with her Polly Pockets than submit to soap and water.

So you give her a little option to smooth her way to bathing. "Ava, babes," you say casually, "do you want to give your Polly Pocket a bath too or just take a bath alone?" You'd be surprised how often the wee donkeys will suddenly agree to your plan; after all, they have had a say in the matter. If she's playing with, say, Grandma's heirloom china doll from the old country (under supervision, of course), obviously you're not going to suggest toting it along in the tub. So then you, savvy mommy, come up with another win-win scenario, creating a choice for your child. "Ava, do you want to run the purple bubbles or Aiden's green 'Incredible Hulk' bubbles?" "Ava, do you want Mom to read you the *Olivia* book while you're in the bath, or do you want to listen to your *Little Mermaid* tape?" You get the picture.

She may very well say, "I don't like those choices," which happens around here with stubborn son number two sometimes. "Well, I understand that," you can reply sympathetically, "but those are the two choices right now." Usually if you make them enticing enough, your child will go along with the options available. The key is giving her little choices that allow her the sense of control she desperately wants and also teach her some decision-making and cooperation skills. Ava would rather play with her dolls, true, but she so badly needs a bath that you picked this battle to "fight." Make it a non-fight instead by finessing, not forcing, the situation.

Unless, Of Course . . .

Your little one really has no choice in the matter. This is a tricky situation because it's so easy to slip into the do-you-want-to mode without thinking it through. Occasionally there will be times for which there are no options. "Do you want to leave the wading pool now?" gives the little missy the idea she has a say in the matter, which she doesn't. "It's time to leave now," spoken firmly yet cheerfully, is the way to go when you need her to make the right choice. What you can do in this case is grease the wheels. Give several pep talks about how important it will be to leave the pool when Mom says it's time, and then give warnings about half

Mr. Dress-Up Was Right

When we were small, you Americans had Mr. Rogers as your sage friend, and we Canadians had Mr. Dress-Up as our kind, gentle, wise television companion. One of the capstones of the *Mr. Dress-Up* program was his "tickle trunk," a magical trunk full of dress-up clothes meant for imaginative play. One day Mr. Dress-Up would transform himself into a brave, armored knight; the next day he'd be a swashbuckling pirate. There was no limit to the worlds he and his puppet friends could go to with a little help from a great costume and a sprinkle of fantasy.

My mom turned an old goldenrod clothes hamper into our own tickle trunk, and inside were endless hours of creative play. An aunt of mine was a department-store model, and she donated her glamorous castoffs to my costume collection. I would spend my days drowning in gold-sequined sheaths and tottering around on much-too-big heels.

Turns out Mr. Dress-Up and Mom were onto something:

"Child development experts agree that dress-up play not only stimulates imagination, it can also be tracked to improved

an hour before, fifteen minutes before, ten minutes before, and five minutes before you leave. Preparing her will mean the difference between a child who is shocked, upset, and furious and one who is disappointed—it's never fun to leave a super-cool place—but more subdued.

vocabulary and social skills. Research shows that children who engage in this type of imaginative, open-ended play are more creative thinkers who eventually mature into better problem solvers. Role-play helps teach children about cooperation and taking turns, and as a result it encourages confidence and socialization. Research also tells us that children who are encouraged in imaginative play prove to be more creative, have a richer vocabulary, are less impulsive and aggressive and often become leaders with their playmates."[2]

You can create your own "tickle trunk" at home with an old laundry hamper, a rubber storage container, or any sturdy box. Fill it with old bridesmaid dresses, Halloween costumes purchased at consignment stores (only four to five dollars, but you have to hit the right season), dollar-store jewels, feather boas, swords and other accoutrements, Daddy's old ties, and so on. You can also discover unique (read "bizarre") sartorial elements at your neighborhood Goodwill store. These are the wide-eyed wonder years, so let's encourage the wonder, spark the creativity, and fuel the fancy inside our preschoolers' boundless imaginations!

For the Hundredth Time

When you've zeroed in on the big fish you want to fry and learned to let go of the many "little fish," get used to frying those biggies many times a day for many days.

"Boys don't hit girls." You want to impart this lesson in the worst way, knowing it's a big one.

"Don't talk back to grown-ups." You desire to instill this message in your child, knowing that kind of respect will stand him in good stead during school years and beyond.

"We are kind to people." You preach and teach this moral in a myriad of ways as you shape his character. You dearly want this bullheaded boy of yours to learn sensitivity, for his sake and for others' sakes.

Redundancy works like nothing else. Say it once, say it a thousand times if necessary. Be a broken record on the things that truly matter. Pick your battles well, and someday you'll be rewarded with a son who is gentle with the females in his life, who is respectful of his college professors and bosses, and who stops and helps that little old lady cross the street, just because it's the right thing to do.

FUN THINGS

"Um, Doctor, I Can Explain"

Ashley had a bloody nose, so I stuck part of a Kleenex partially up her nose. Two minutes later I noticed the tissue was gone, so we headed to the doctor's office. Two hours later I got to see her chart. It read, "Mom stuffed tissue up nose. Removed with tweezers." Boy, did I feel great about that one!—Amy

6

THINGS THAT GO BUMP
IN THE NIGHT

Soothing your monster-freaked little one

"WHEN MAX WAS four or five he woke up really afraid and told us he had dreamed that Auntie Jen was trying to scare him and making faces in his dream," says Alanna. "He was really afraid of this memory of her in his dream and had trouble going to sleep for nap and for night for quite some time."

Now, Max's dad is my cousin Rick, which makes Auntie Jen my cousin too. I was surprised when I heard this story, because I know how beautiful and gentle Jennifer is, and how close she and her precious first nephew are. How could Max possibly have had a scary dream about the aunt who loves him so much? But just as we grown-ups have nightmares, so our kids also suffer from twisted, often terrifying dreams. The only difference is that we know, for example, that we were not actually falling off a building while we slept.

Preschoolers are more victimized by their bad dreams—and other fears—because they can't yet tell the difference between fantasy and reality. And because bad dreams most often happen during the light stage of sleep (REM), tiny tots are easily jolted out of sleep and into sheer fright. "Bad dreams are the most common reason for sleep disturbances in children between 2 and 5 years old," says Dr. William Sears.[1] And when innocent little Max looks around his darkened room, he fully believes the visage of his aunt, distorted like a creepy fun-house mirror in his dream, may be out to snatch him away from his room, home, and most of all, you.

Monsters, the boogeyman, creepy shadows, ominously lumpy clumps of clothes or stuffed animals—in the dark of night, all of these are valid reasons for your preschooler to flee his room, wailing in fear. It's easy to dismiss our fright-filled munchkin when he comes to us utterly convinced there's a giant octopus in his room. But our terrified child needs to be taken seriously, because he truly cannot distinguish between the towel hanging on his bedside chair and the horrible ghost conjured by his vivid imagination.

Rick and Alanna took Max seriously, and their care paid off:

> We showed Max a picture of Auntie Jen on her wedding day, holding him and smiling. We assured him that he knows Auntie Jen *very* well, and that she would never do anything to scare him. All of this still did not help. Rick was blessed with a very wise idea, which I believe was from the Lord. He suggested that we let Max tell Auntie Jen about his

dream. I talked to her first, giving her a little background of the situation, and then we let him describe the dream to her. She lovingly told him how much he meant to her, and that she would never do anything, ever, to hurt or scare him. Max has slept peacefully ever since.

Chasing Away the Boogeyman

Experts say that by first or second grade, kids know the difference between ghosts and towels, or nightmares and real life. But for now, try the following monster busters and see if you, like Alanna, can't banish those funny things that go bump in the night.

Find the Monster Trigger

Ask your scaredy-cat to describe her nightmares so you can try to get at the source.

"Josephine is absolutely freaked by anything scary, so we avoid frightening books, videos, and stories at all costs," says Mary Jo. "She has yet to awaken from a bad dream, although she has claimed to have had 'bad dreams' about cows—seven skinny and seven fat. (You may recognize this story about a certain pharaoh in the book of Genesis.) We don't believe it's an 'original' dream!"

Evidently Josephine picked up on a Sunday school story that got blown out of proportion in her dreams. (It doesn't have to make sense. Remember Max's scary dreams about Aunt Jen?) Even age-appropriate TV shows, DVDs, or books can hold pictures that morph into sinister visions at night. When you get to the bottom of your child's bad

73

dreams, talk about it in the light of day, and hopefully this will help normalize the images for her.

Watch Out for Stressors

Could there be stress triggers in your child's life? Kids are stressed out by things that might not phase us one bit. Consider possibly unsettling events in your child's life, such as a recent move, death of a pet (even a fish), starting preschool, or having an older sibling (and playmate) begin a new routine, like all-day school. Anxiety during the day often results in strange, unsettling dreams at night for preschoolers, just as it does for adults.

De-Creep Dottie's Room

Look at her room through her four-year-old eyes. Could that hanging quilt look scary surrounded by dark shadows? Is the closet door slightly ajar? My kids both went through phases of being scared of what was in their closets. Closing the door to the possibilities usually worked. How about that oversized teddy bear, sitting so jauntily in a child's rocking chair? With limited vision, Teddy may loom large and take on monstrous qualities. If a night-light helps, by all means plug it in. And make sure she has her beloved stuffed lamb or doll close at hand for moral support.

Enlist a Famous Friend

"All of the sudden a few months ago, Maddy became afraid of her room at night. She would not state any specific fears, just that she was afraid, and she started waking up frequently during the night," says Jen P. "In desperate need of sleep and wanting her to feel better, she and I went to Meijer to find a night-light. We found one shaped like a star. Maddy's favorite show is *Dora the Explorer*. Dora is very brave and catches 'magic stars' on her trips. So the star night-light became a 'magic star' that made Maddy brave like Dora—and voilà! She's back to sleeping through the night again!"

Tickle Away the Trepidation

"I recently created the tickle monster, and when Gabbi is afraid I reassure her that the only monster I know of is the tickle monster," says Jen T. "And of course he has to come out of hiding to tickle her! We laugh and giggle for a while, and very soon the fear is gone. I then say a bedtime prayer with her and ask her guardian angel to watch over her."

Spray Away the Spooks

This one's a classic because it works. Fill a spray bottle with water (you and your artsy kid might even decorate the bottle with green and black yarn, puce-yellow paint, and foam shapes of spiders or bats), and spritz the room with "monster spray." Just like when you spray for bugs, when you spray for monsters, they are gone. A flashlight also worked for my son Jonah, who could beam his light on any corner of the room that seemed scary. Trust me, novelty works with the monster-phobics!

Lull Away the Lonelies

"Ashley hasn't really had a bad dream yet that she has reported to us; however, quite often she has come into our room in the middle of the night to report that she is lonely," says Amy. "We crawl out of bed and turn on her lullaby CD. This usually fixes the problem."

Bat Away the Bugs

"Adrielle was convinced she saw bugs all over her room," says Cheryl. "Of course, they were imaginary. So we gave her a bug swatter and told her to swat any bugs that she saw. She seemed to feel more comfortable when she had a 'weapon.' Naturally, Bruce and I did our fair share of bug swatting too."

Pray for Peace

"When we pray together before bed, we always ask the Lord to keep the kids' minds at peace," says Alanna. "Often when the boys are sleeping, I like to go in and pray over them the verse 'Thou wilt keep him in perfect peace, whose mind is stayed on thee' (Isa. 26:3 KJV). Bennett asks us to pray with him that he won't have any bad dreams. As far as I can recall, the nights that we've prayed that extra prayer for and with him, he hasn't had any bad dreams. In the morning we thank God for honoring the desire of our dear little son's heart."

Don't Let Your Child Sleep with You

Cheryl advises,

Don't even do that once, or you and your spouse will be sleeping like an H with your kid being the horizontal line between you, shoving you to the edge of the bed! When

THINGS THAT GO BUMP IN THE NIGHT

Nathanael was younger, he was terrified of thunderstorms. I would usually go into his room, do my best to calm him, and then sleep with him in his twin bed for a while, and he'd be fine. Adrielle sleeps in a toddler bed, and I'm *so* not crawling into that bed. When she has an honest-to-goodness

Just a Spoonful of Medicine

Speaking of bedtime, often that's when we need to give medicine to our child. How can we get that pink stuff (or worse, white stuff!) down the hatch with a minimum of sputtering and stress? Here are some great ideas.

Hand him the spoon after you've poured out the correct dosage and let him take it himself. Maybe it's a control thing and being in charge will motivate him to gulp it down.

Have a "race" to see if he can finish his medicine before you're done singing "Jingle Bells" or "Do Your Ears Hang Low?"

Literally, add a spoonful of sugar or honey, and make a big production out of mixing it in. It worked for Mary Poppins, after all.

"We pretend that my son is the patient and I am the doctor. He tells me what's wrong, and I tell him we have just the thing to help fix him. He takes his medicine with no questions asked."[2]

77

bad dream and she's not just stalling about bed, often all I have to do is say, "I'm sorry you had a bad dream, honey. But you're OK, and Daddy and I will be right in the next room. Do you have your blankie?" Seventy-five percent of the time that's enough for her.

Do ease her anxiety, though. Let your little one sleep on a mattress at the foot of your bed or beside it if you feel comfortable with doing so. Or let her cozy up to an older sibling until she feels safe again in her own bed.

FUN THINGS

Overheard at Preschool, Part 2

Kayla: "My hair is thick because I got highlights."
Teacher: "Where did you get highlights?"
Kayla: "From heaven."

Andrew: "No glittering [littering]!"

Kayla: "My mom got to China by digging a hole in her backyard when she was a little girl. We tried to get there in my backyard once, but we only got worms."

Emily: "I can sleep and talk at the same time!"

Teacher: "Come here, my little angels."
Sam: "Angels? Oh brrutherrrr!"

Justin: "Hey, I learned this song from a funeral."

Kate: "I've changed my name to Katie Ballerina."

Basil: "God is God and Jesus is Jesus. He's big. At our house we know that."

Gets and Goodness

Deprogramming your material girls (and boys)

Right before my eyes, my son was turning into a greedy "gimme" boy, barely glancing at the freshly opened Christmas present before swiveling around to look for more loot. Jonah's birthday was December 6, almost three weeks before Christmas, and he was completely jaded to the thrill and joy of receiving gifts by the time the holiday came around. I felt sick as I witnessed his transformation from sweet little boy to gift hog.

Then Ezra came of the age where he understands that he's supposed to get hyped up about unwrapping the presents under the tree. His birthday? December 19, a mere six days before the next gift-a-palooza. (Guess when our baby Phoebe, adopted from Korea, was born? December 30! God sure has a sense of humor.) Ezra's eyeballs were glazed over with abject avarice, and we still had two gift-giving occasions to go before the yuletide was a wrap. Ez's life during those days between his birthday and Christmas revelries entailed spinning one big lazy Susan filled with presents for him. My boys were glutted with gifts, some they didn't want and most they didn't need.

Something had to be done, I resolved, before my children became deadened to the sweetness of unwrapping a carefully chosen, lovingly given gift.

Later, I'll tell you some of the solutions I've come up with to guard my boys' hearts (and the heart of their sister when she actually cares about what's inside a box) from soul-rotting greed that can infiltrate the most well-meaning household around Noel time. My preschool panel had some fantastic, hard-won ideas as well for yanking our kids from Christmas covetousness and pointing them to the deeper blessings of the season.

My children all have December birthdays. (You're laughing at me, aren't you? Well, let me warn you: if you haven't completed your family yet, avoid having sex in March unless you want my fate!) This fact brings the issue of curbing materialism into sharp focus. But you and I know that molding our kids' hearts to be generous, to be others centered, and to steer them away from becoming crazed little consumers is an all-year endeavor.

"Mommy, Look! Will You Buy Me That Junk?"

Unless you have a live-in nanny or a husband who works at home and loves nothing more than to stop what he's doing and be on Daddy duty, you will probably often shop with your darlings. And before long they will reach that magical age when they are suddenly able to spot a wanted item from amazingly far away. It's then up to us as responsible parental units to nip the consumerism in its greedy little bud.

The Big Pep Talk Is Key

With these squirts, you must set ground rules well before you even get to the store, or you're in trouble. "Listen up, Harry-doodle," you begin. "It's fun to go shopping with Mommy, isn't it? Mom's got a list of groceries to buy, so you won't be getting any toys or treats today, OK, buddy? But if you're a super-good boy, Mommy will let you pick out one food treat, like a special ice cream or cereal. I wonder if they have that new Incredibles cereal we saw on the commercial? That looks yummy, doesn't it?" Finding that one item keeps them engaged and lets them practice the art of prioritizing.

Then you ask Harry to reiterate what it is he will be allowed to pick out and what he is not getting on that particular day (i.e., a toy). Just make yourself as clear as you can so there's no confusion when Harry spies something that is cool, such as an overpriced Bob the Builder Mylar balloon.

Expeditions to Target or Wal-Mart are inevitably harder, stocked as they are with all manner of enticement for shoppers young and old. Again, verbalize what it is you are going to buy, then when the inevitable request comes to buy him something, say, "Sorry, it's not on the list."

And it's perfectly fine to state your intentions of not buying him a single thing. "Harry, today we are just going to

81

run in and out of the store, and this time we are just buying some soap and a birthday gift for Grandpa, OK?"

Amy says, "We don't usually buy Ashley things when we go to Target or anywhere. She knows that she can earn things by behaving well and treating others well. When she does receive something new, it is for a reason. For example, it is for her birthday, becoming potty trained, and other major milestones."

Or you can make a speech about how your child may touch something of interest and look at it for a while, but on that day, you aren't buying it. "Adrielle will frequently want to see or hold a toy in the store," says Cheryl. "Sometimes I'll let her, but I always tell her, 'You can hold it, but we're not buying it.' I'll let her hold it for a few aisles, and then we'll put it back. If she really wants it, I tell her, 'We'll put it on your Christmas list.'"

I used to buy my guys little trinkets sometimes because I love giving gifts, and Jonah's "love language" is gifts. I figured, it's $1.99 and life is short, so why not? I've curbed this habit, though, because the kids were starting to expect a little something on every shopping expedition. It's a great thing, I've learned, to impart the value of going without.

Where the Rubber Meets the Road

Sometimes you just have to say no in the heat of the moment, which means your tot may well blow a gasket right there in the checkout lane. "No, sweetheart, not today. It's too expensive, and besides, you don't need another plastic dinosaur right now. You've still got one in your room somewhere."

82

Of course, your enraged triceratops aficionado couldn't care less that he has a dino at home (*where* is the million-dollar question). He wants one right *now*! And this is where the rubber meets the road, because it's difficult and embarrassing to listen to him caterwauling in public, and it would be infinitely easier to grab the thing and mute the screaming. But you want to teach him that he can't have everything he wants, and this is a fantastic time to do so.

Is Allowance a Good Idea for Preschoolers?

Eager to instill the precept of solid money management to my firstborn son, we began giving Jonah an allowance at the age of four. What I didn't know then but was quick to learn was that at age four, he was too young to comprehend the idea of his own money. Often he wouldn't even care about the dollar we gave him, and I would end up washing it in a pair of pants. When he turned six, though, he was much more capable of understanding money and even the idea of saving for something. With Ezra, who's four, I tally up what he would have gotten with his "own" money, had we given him an allowance, and I do from time to time allow him to buy a little something, especially when Jonah is spending his allowance.

I recently paid Ez one dollar to pick up broken summer toys that were revealed when the snow melted in our backyard. Interestingly, he eagerly did his chore with great gusto, but when the compensation was remitted, so to speak, he stuffed the money in his pocket and forgot about it. Next time we go to the dollar store, I'm going to remind him of his dollar (now in my purse), and that he earned a dollar-store toy with his own money. Overall, though, I agree with the camp that advises parents to hold out on an allowance before first grade. There are other ways to teach a preschooler about the worth of a dollar.

Giving instead of Getting

Friends of mine are enthusiastic boosters of their children tithing. "Money to save, money to keep, and money for Jesus," is their motto when doling out $5 at the beginning of the month. While I agree wholeheartedly with the concept, again I think preschoolers lack the understanding to save or tithe. "The amount you give a young child is so small that further division renders it meaningless," says money expert Diane Harris. "As for charity money, the idea of donating to a worthy cause is too abstract for literal minded youngsters." True, 10 percent of five dollars is fifty cents. So why not drill in the principle of tithing at an early age, even if it just amounts to a pittance? Because they just don't get it. And besides, there are other more effective ways to impart the idea of giving to church or charity. "To foster my children's charitable instincts, I had them accompany me to a soup kitchen to hand over turkeys at Thanksgiving and choose toys to donate to the local toy drive around the holidays," Harris writes.[1] It's vitally important, however, to shape your child's view of money so he knows that it's not just for buying stuff but for helping people and even for advancing God's work. He's too little to understand the dollars and cents of it, but if you talk about where the family's money is going—to help the Tsunami kids, for Uncle Alex in Yugoslavia, so he can tell people about Jesus, to buy the displaced family at church some groceries—he'll learn as he grows that your money and later his money can be put to good use.

Mute the Commercials

Nothing fuels materialism like television, with enticing, irresistible commercials aimed at hooking pint-sized buyers. I try to steer my kids to watching public television for this reason whenever their favorite shows, *Higglytown Heroes* (Ezra) or *Jimmy Neutron* (Jonah), are not airing. This is a small thing, but it makes a difference. "It helps that we do not have cable TV and live in an area that has terrible reception," says Cheryl. "We watch videos, which don't have commercials, and what they don't see, they don't want."

Coping with Fairy Grandparents

Your parents or in-laws shower your child with toys and cash on birthdays, holidays, and just-because days. How do you ask them, tactfully, to keep spoilage to a dull roar, especially when you are attempting to raise enlightened, generous children whose toy boxes are not stacked to the skies?

First, we have to keep in mind what may be going on behind Grandma's parade of gifts. She means well, but she may be trying to make up for something she wasn't able to give you. And besides, if Grandma won't spoil you, who will?

It's not a bad problem to have, but if Granny and Gramps are overdoing it a wee bit (was that toy replica of Donald Trump's jag really necessary?), it's time for some very diplomatic moves.

Make sure you and your husband are on the same page, especially if it's his parents who go crazy in the gift department. Your first tactical maneuver could be to tell your parents or in-laws that your child already has so many nice toys and clothes and that your new family policy is to cut back a bit. Say it nicely, of course! Use a light touch. "You know, Mother Snodgrass, we don't want to ruin her completely for marriage! Look at all of little Molly's clothes! I am starting to feel sorry for her future husband! Maybe we should all restrain ourselves just a tad here. She's already the best-dressed girl in preschool."

Suggesting alternative (and less materialistic) ways to satisfy Grandma's spending urges is good too. Says Carol,

> My family was out of control! They totally believed in quantity, not quality. After joking that pretty soon we'd have to live in the garage because of all the toys, we finally suggested that they give us money for dance or violin lessons for our daughter or hockey equipment for our son. We really talk it up, the fact that Grandma and Grandpa paid for these lessons or equipment, and the kids have thanked them more than once. We also make a point to tell them how much the kids are benefiting from these "experiential" gifts—so much more than toys they don't play with that much. I think Bryan's parents also enjoy going to a dance recital or hockey game, knowing they facilitated these experiences for their grandchildren.

Another idea is to involve the grandparents in your quandary. Don't blame them specifically, of course, but do mention how you are getting concerned with the vast number of toys that are piling up at the house. "What did you do when Jason was little?" you might ask your mother-in-law one day over coffee. "How did you control all that stuff a child accumulates?" Asking for advice on how to handle stuff overload opens up dialogue, helps grandparents realize they may be going overboard, and makes them feel as if they can be part of the solution, not just the source of the problem.

When Visions of Sugarplums Rot Their Heads (and Souls)

"One side of our family has no restraint at all in terms of giving too many gifts, especially at Christmas," says Jen P. "One year, Maddy was asleep on the floor of the living room, and certain family members were waking her up to open more presents!"

Wise Men Say . . .

Christmas can be the most difficult time of year to teach our wide-eyed wonder boys and girls that it's better to give than to receive. As I said earlier, my boys were overwhelmed by the sheer volume of new items that piled up around them at Christmastime. They were numbed by all the toys, and the situation was made worse by the fact that they had hardly gotten any play out of birthday gifts when they were faced with a slew of new toys! As parents, Doyle and I had to act fast, or the beauty, peace, and meaning of Christ's birth would have been completely lost under a heap of playthings and the frenzied accumulation thereof.

Two years ago, we presented a new framework for Christmas presents. Each of us, grown-ups included, received three gifts, just like Jesus, who was given gold, frankincense, and myrrh by the three wise men. We also followed the Victorian custom of "something you want, something you need, and a surprise." (Ann, who also follows this tradition, heard it as a poem: "something to wear, something to read, something they want, and something they need." The "something you need" designation is great because this allows you to buy winter boots or coats or a bookshelf—something practical and something you'd be buying anyway—to put under the tree.)

I've had few strokes of brilliance in my mothering journey, but, folks, this was one of them. We love the simplicity of the three gifts, and the logic of the plan appeals to a child's mind. Why should they get more presents than Jesus, after all? Also, knowing our family gift exchange only makes up less than half of their total haul (Grandma's just itching to throw more gifts at them!), we often choose fairly inexpensive or educational gifts, anticipating the toy deluge that is to come. And no, the kids are not deprived one bit by three gifts, even counting the unexciting snow pants they unwrapped. They didn't break into song and dance, but they were surprisingly happy with their practical present anyway.

Is Santa for Real?

I for one dreaded the question, because it signaled to me an end to the wide-eyed wonder years. Childhood is so short already. That brilliant window of time—where kids believe that woodland creatures really do have tea parties—closes a little more each day. And then there's Santa, in all his holly, jolly glory—so kind, so giving, such a grand pal to children who watch for his sleigh on Christmas Eve. We focus on Christ's birth, above all else, but we also include a little Santa in our celebrations. We leave cookies and milk for him (this year St. Nick had to make do with buttermilk, so I'm not sure he'll be back!), and we warble "Rudolph" at the top of our lungs. If you're like me, and you want to preserve the awe and mystery as long as possible, answer the inevitable question with great care. "What do you think, honey?" opens the door for clarification. Maybe an older brother has already let the Kris Kringle cat out of the bag. But maybe your tot will just keep believing in Santa anyway.

Some kids don't want to know the truth. They just want to talk about what they know now. If they do want to know, break it to them gently. In either case, be sure to check out the marvelous book *Santa, Are You for Real?* by Harold Myra. This book tells a simple story of the real Santa—St. Nicholas—his love for Jesus, and his generous secret gifts to the poor. The final page is open ended, so there are no shocking revelations to worry about.

Ho Ho Ho: The Preschool Panel

Check out some of the nifty, gifty brain waves my panel contributed (you'll love Jen P.'s idea!). Their traditions aim to bridle rampant yuletide consumerism, emphasize time together, and answer the burning question, How do we as moms highlight Christ's birth, giving the miracle of miracles—not presents!—top billing?

Johana: From our parents, we are starting to ask for family memberships to the zoo or children's museum instead of gifts. We are also starting to make "coupons" a bigger part of our gift giving within our family. For example, giving a coupon for Mom to clean up a kid's room for the day, or one for a date with Dad where the kid picks the spot, or one for a special dinner cooked by Mom featuring a favorite meal.

Mary: We ask for "educational" and "experience" gifts instead of toys. We especially appreciate books that help develop reading skills, craft kits that encourage hands-on activity, and gift certificates that allow us to experience things together, such as going out for ice cream or bowling. This doesn't mean my children never get toys (they get plenty!), but it does help reduce the number of new things we bring into our home each year.[2]

Mary Jo: Because the toys from our extended family are enough, we have decided to give our girls very small, simple gifts—one or two usually educational in nature, like sewing cards. We heard of an idea that we plan to start next year. The girls will have a limit of a certain number of "big" gifts (say three), and if they get more, we will have them choose three favorites and donate the rest to children who do not have many toys.

Ann: Dan and I give Adam and Ingrid an average of two books each Christmas, one Christmas story and one other book. In the weeks leading up to Christmas I always feel that this is not enough, but by the time we are even halfway through Christmastime, I realize that our small children are completely overwhelmed by everything they have gotten from grandparents and extended family. Two books are definitely enough! I am glad Dan helped me stick to our plan. I also often make or purchase matching pj's for the entire family for Christmas Eve. This is fun for me and carries on a tradition from my childhood of getting new pj's each Christmas Eve.

Ann also gave a list of fresh ideas for experiential gifts:

- Memberships for the whole family to the zoo, a botanical garden, the children's museum, a gym, or a state park
- Prepaid lessons for swimming, tennis, dance, skating, or music
- Tickets for a special outing, like *Lollypops* symphony tickets, the ballet, or a children's play
- Movie tickets for the whole family
- A gift certificate for an overnight with grandparents so Mom and Dad can have a night away!

Jen P.: We limit what we get Maddy, and because we always have limited it, so far she doesn't know the difference and is very excited by the few things she gets. We also try to teach her in ways she can understand about people having less than we do. A great thing that my father started doing when Maddy was born was make donations to Heifer International in Maddy's name. The organization gives livestock to people in poverty with the money donated. Then the person whose name it was donated in gets a card explaining what benefits the livestock will have for the family. It has pictures of the animals given and is very kid friendly. Maddy doesn't totally get the whole picture, but she understands she gave a flock of chicks to some people who didn't have much!

Jen T.: This was the first year for Gabbi that Christmas became "What am I getting for Christmas?" and not "What is Christmas about?" or "What could we help others with?" I know that I am partly responsible for the beginning of this attitude, but it was also accentuated by my mother-in-law.

So when my mother-in-law was taking care of Gabbi one day, I brought over a bunch of books relating to Christmas and the birth of Jesus for her to read to Gabbi. It seemed that after that day Gabbi was much improved, making birthday cards for baby Jesus, wanting to make a cake for his birthday, and so on. I know it wasn't a complete success, but I feel that a good seed was sown, and we can be more careful next year to put more focus on helping others.

Diane Harris, the money expert we heard from earlier regarding tithing, weighs in with these inspired thoughts about accentuating family traditions and "homemade" gifts that will knit your clan closer:

On the first night of Hanukkah, my husband, children [Rachel and Michael], and I draw names out of a hat, and then we're responsible for providing that family member with some kind of service. Last year Rachel drew Michael and promised to make his bed for two weeks. Rachel, Michael, and I spend every Christmas Eve day baking together, with holiday tunes blasting in the background. Later, all four of us sing carols together. My kids still get too much stuff for the holidays, and they love it. But I no longer worry that the season is all about gifts for them.[3]

Get on Board the World of Wooden Trains

When Jonah turned three, Doyle and I bought him a wooden train set, which we set up in a figure eight on his bedroom floor, and watched the play begin. At the time, we didn't know the legacy of little boys and wooden trains, that they'd been scooting engines and cars around tracks for more than a century. All we knew is that Jonah was mesmerized by the train table at Pooh's Corner, our local children's bookstore. He was fascinated with action, self-powered torque, controlling the train cars, and figuring out how the little choo-choo got from point A to point B.

Experts say wooden train play—or any train play where a child's hands rather than batteries put the trains into action—helps the players grow in cognitive skills, imagination, and hand-eye coordination. And besides the developmental value, preschoolers are enamored with the tiny engines and cars that are perfect for their little hands. At the peak of creative and open-ended play, little conductors can enter into a world of motion and action they control, and they love it! One more benefit of wooden trains: the simple, sturdy construction is the antithesis of "junky" toys and can be passed down to younger siblings or cousins, or even kept for the next generation of junior engineers.[4]

De-Junk—You'll Feel like a Million Bucks

So the toys piled up anyway, despite your best efforts. What do you do with all of the stuff? Hide a few items for later rotation, or, like Mary Jo, choose the big three popular items and give the rest away. Make sure your tots are involved in the process so it actually means something to them. Bring them to the homeless shelter or to Goodwill with you. This experience will have far more effect on them than if you had simply packed up their extra toys and they never saw them again.

You can de-junk anytime during the year if you feel the house will soon topple over from the weight of too many Tonka trucks. As a family, we just filled three huge Rubbermaid containers with books, CDs, movies, clothes, and oodles of toys—we found we had four big yellow Tonka trucks in our possession! Two trucks went into the MOPS rummage sale along with all the other "treasures," and two remain. It felt amazing—freeing and cleansing and rejuvenating—as if a big burden had been taken off my shoulders. I highly recommend it. You'll feel like a new woman, and your kids will gain the blessings of giving and living a slightly simpler life.

FUN THINGS

How to Grocery Shop with Your Three-Year-Old

1. Wait while your child decides between the regular old carts and the newfangled plastic-vehicle-attached cart. (Wonder why this always takes so long, because he always chooses the car thing.)

2. Say something innocuous in response to your child's request for a six-dollar Mylar balloon in the shape of Scooby Doo's head. "We have balloons at home, honey." Hope it's true. (Wish the grocery store didn't carry hideously expensive balloons.)

3. Grab bananas, apples, grapes, premade salad, and other items from the produce section. Stop the cart so Junior can rip off a twist tie, knowing this will buy you two minutes of serenity as he bends it in different ways.

4. Use this two-minute span to linger at the gourmet salad dressing display, reading labels and comparing the carb content of the "Tuscany Sun-Ripened Tomato/Dried Cherry" and "Valencia Onion/Feta Cheese/Spanish Olive Oil" dressings.

5. "Mommy! I dropped the twisty!" Oops, your time is up, so you press on to dairy. (Later you'll snag the same store-brand ranch dressing you always get.)

6. Knowing the only way Mr. Twisty is going to eat vegetables is if they are covertly tucked under masses of mild cheddar shreds, you note with glee that shredded cheese is on sale. (You ignore his pleas for Shrek yogurt tubes.)

7. The two of you make your obligatory stop at the fresh lobster tank to visit with the happy, oblivious lobster family. (While your son checks out the crustaceans, you loiter four feet away at the magazine stand, speed-flipping through a glossy decorating magazine.)

8. Cruising at high speed down the cereal aisle, you deflect half a dozen requests for sugary cereals, all with various movie-related motifs. No to Spider-Man, the Incredibles, Nemo, and Bob the Builder. No especially to the brand where the piece-of-junk watch "inside" is actually a mail-

95

order offer, good with three proofs of purchase. (Recall with a shudder the last time you explained that the toy was not *actually* in the box but was sitting in a warehouse somewhere, awaiting your three UPC codes.)

9. When you're sure he's not looking, fling a couple boxes of Cheerios in the cart.

10. Half an hour into the shopping expedition, begin fielding grumbles from your tyke about wanting to be inside the cart since he is sick of the plastic car thing and wants to see more stuff. Silently review safety info, which strongly suggests a three-year-old should not be in the cart as he might lean too far out and crack his head open. Tell him, "You made the choice to drive the truck, so that's where you'll stay for today." Know this is not the end of it by any stretch of the imagination.

11. Begin speeding up as you see the fruit juice snacks approaching. Faster, faster, faster . . . you're zooming down the aisle when your tyke notices—naturally—the blurred vision of Incredibles-themed snacks. You screech on your brakes and have a prolonged discussion about all the different snacks available and how your household really needs only one box. (The snacks will all be gone in forty-eight hours anyway.)

12. Your preschooler begins leaning out of the cart, dragging his fingers, orangutan-like, on the floor.

13. You begin badgering him to stop dragging his fingers, all the while keeping one eye on him and one eye on the meat counter. And, of course, one eye on other carts because you don't want to crash the cart-attached-to-plastic-car into the blue-haired lady asking the butcher about the availability of cod loin. (Yes, you are now out of eyes.)

14. Realize you didn't know cod had loins.

15. Cruise through frozen foods, wishing you could loiter awhile in the low-fat frozen entrees section. Toss in waffles, broccoli, and ice cream, ignoring your tot's pleas for the black and green popsicles shaped like the Hulk. (Recall with a wince the time you practically marinated your son's T-shirt—stained with black ice from a similar concoction—in spot cleanser, only to end up with a grayish blob.)

16. With one arm, restrain your child from leaning out of the cart/car thing, and with the other arm, try to catch a falling can of tuna. At the same moment, your child grabs some shark fruit snacks from the display, causing a bunch to topple over. Too late you realize you are out of arms.

17. Picking up the snacks, you grumpily tell your son he has lost his right to choose a sucker at the checkout.

18. Endure whining as you speed-cruise your cart through the baking aisle, the detergent aisle, and the coffee and tea aisle, chucking items into the cart as fast as you can.

19. Tap your foot impatiently as you wait behind a woman with seven hundred items in her cart. Your son has ratcheted up the whining to new heights. Stifle a scream when the woman realizes she has forgotten item 701. Wonder if the alien family on the tabloid would like to adopt your child.

20. Vow to drive across town for your next grocery run to the swanky area where the fancy, overpriced market offers free child care.

8

"PLEASE UNCLAMP YOURSELF FROM MY LEG"

Helping your little cling-ons

"BEN SEEMS TO be so sensitive to other people," says Brenna. "He's so scared in new situations and so easily overwhelmed by new people and situations. He doesn't know what to expect and feels out of control! With Little Stars [church preschool class] or MOPS nursery or any-where else where Mom and Dad are apart from him, there are major tears and he gets freak-out clingy. Ben generally gets over it (if I have to leave while he's still crying) and ends up having a good time, but the fear is still there for the next time."

Does anything rip out a mom's heart like having to pry her wailing child from her leg, turn her back, and walk away from the unbearably sad sound of her child's cries? Arrgh! When this happens with Ez, I'm always just itching to rush back, scoop him up, and never leave him again. Alas, separation anxiety is one of the banes of motherhood.

You're a Good Mom, Even If Junior Is Clingy

If you happen to have one of those turbo-social tykes who wiggles out of your arms so he can run and play with his friends, count yourself lucky. Jonah was and is a party animal who never looks back when I drop him off, with the exception of the first days of preschool, kindergarten, and first grade, when he did kind of hang back with me for a few moments. Sounds crazy, but I treasure those rare times of temerity, those all-too-brief moments in my social son's childhood when he stuck close to Mom for a little extra security.

But Ezra is a little cling-on sometimes, and I know how exasperating and heart-wrenching it can be to deal with separation anxiety, aka clinging. Many children go through this as a normal part of their development. Preschoolers are discovering they are separate from you, maybe for the first time. And some kids, like Jonah, adjust quickly to new situations, while others, like Ben and Ezra, are more fearful, more cautious about plunging in. Jodi's twins, Eliana and Lillian, are like this too. "Both my children are very clingy," she says. "I reassure them and pray with them often. We ask God to give them courage and to make them feel brave. It can be difficult to have two clingy children, but the positive side to it is that I always know where they are! I never have the fear of losing them or of them wandering off."

There you are—a silver lining to clinginess! But seriously, it could wreck your day to leave your sweetie when she so clearly does not want to be left. So how can you smooth those bumpy days when your child is clamped to your legs and won't let go?

First, get inside her little brain for a minute and consider what's going on behind all this angst. And for all of you fellow neurotic moms out there, what's going on is *not* that you're a bad mother, even though you see other kids detaching breezily from their mothers. Like we've established, some kids are simply more cautious. This doesn't mean you have failed at some key aspect of your job as her mom. It doesn't mean timid Tia will grow up and fasten herself to you at her graduation open house. It's a personality thing and also a very common stage of development.

Now that we've gotten the "I'm a bad mommy" guilt trip off the table, let's get back to the weaning process. If your child is attending a kids' fitness program at the gym for the first time (you hope to take a dip in the pool yourself), talk it up like crazy. Preschool-age kids need to know what to expect when entering new situations. Don't just plunk the child at the gym, dash off, and hope for the best. Prepare her and get her enthused about the experience. Even better, if you know a fellow member of the program your child is attending, carpool together so she can walk in with a friend.

101

Cling-On Grows Up

Are new places and faces stressful for your reticent one? You'd better believe it, but in this case, a little sweat is a good thing. Suzanne Dixon, M.D., who writes frequently about early childhood development, says,

> Childhood is a period of psychological growth, and that growth is spurred partly by mild to moderate stress. While parents shouldn't strive to eliminate all stress, they should try to understand what's stressing their kids so they can support them through it. By teaching kids that life can be challenging and exciting, we give them the gift of accomplishment, of managing a new task, in the same way we let a baby feed himself when he grabs the spoon. The kitchen (and you) may be worse for the wear, but the baby is better for his achievement.[1]

Your baby will be better off when he finds his way without you, charting unknown territories. (Cue up music for "Climb Every Mountain" sniff, sniff.). You know him better than anyone, and you know his peculiar sensitivities and fears, which is why it kills you to peel him off your waist and leave him somewhere. Look at it this way: because you know that little soul inside and out, you are best qualified to gently but firmly push him into places he doesn't want to go but that are growth-spurring for him. He will adapt, even if it takes awhile. "Ben needs quite a bit of adjustment time before he feels comfortable in most situations," says Brenna. "But after repeated exposure to new places or people, Ben becomes more familiar with them. At some point, he starts to associate some good things with being there that override the fear of being apart from me."

A Rite of Passage

Talk about clingy! Talk about clamping on for dear life! The first day of preschool for Jonah was terrible, so embarrassing. I didn't think they'd ever be able to pry my hands loose from that sand table. ("Um, Mrs. Craker, you're scaring the children. Could you stop wailing now?")

What can I say? That day, I didn't want to leave my baby, his hair slicked back endearingly with gel, hoisting a backpack and lunch box, a little man. So I feigned a coughing spell and made a beeline for the car, blubbering all the way home at the rite of passage we had just experienced. Maybe I was so sad because I knew this was just the first of many doorways he'd go through—without me.

Pathetic, I know. But for most of us moms, it has to be done. Besides our own sentimental seizures, of course, there's the small student-to-be to worry about. If the church nursery causes anxiety, won't preschool be a hard sell? Maybe, maybe not, depending on your kid's personality. But even the most bold and brash little guy or girl may need some encouragement before venturing off into the world of chalk dust and apples for teacher.

Preschool Is Gonna Rock

"Preschool Is Beyond Awesome, Buddy!"

Read books about preschool, and act out what school might be like. Kiddies often work through their anxieties by playing, and pretending they are the teacher and their dolls are the students gives them a sense of control over the situation. Chat about what kinds of activities

103

"Do You Do Windows Too?"

Your preschooler wants to help with the household chores. Oh joy. Yes, the tasks will take twice as long, and you'll have a bit more work for yourself later on. But kids love to help, and the sooner they learn basic skills, the sooner they'll actually be helpful. So here are a few tasks that even three-year-olds can do with just a little tutoring.

Setting and clearing the table. Your tot can help you set and clear the table with more proficiency then you would guess. Grab the plastic or Tupperware plates and cups and show him how to place the plates in front of each chair, then the forks, knives, and so on. Clearing tables is even easier. Ask your mini-domestic to put all

she'll be doing at school. Separation is the most difficult when they don't know what is happening. Buy fun new stickers and have your child place a sticker on a special calendar, marking the days before school begins. Drive by the place fifteen times, excitedly pointing it out: "Look, guys, Chloe's new school!" Drum up as much enthusiasm as you can!

A Cool Lunch Box Goes a Long Way

Shop together for backpacks, clothes, or school supplies. You may not be crazy about the Princess Jasmine top your the dishes in the sink or bring them to you as you load the dishwasher.

Loading and unloading the dishwasher. When he gets a little more savvy in his helping skills, you can give him the MO for loading the dishwasher. You rinse, he loads. To ease into this chore, give your dishwashing boy the job of placing cups in the top row of the machine. While he's helping, he is also learning about shapes and sizes. If you can't stand the thought of a broken dish, consider buying a set of plastic plates and cups for everyday use. When unloading, let him hand you the dishes while you put them away. If any cups turned over during the cycle, let your child empty them into the sink.

preschool girl chooses, but wearing something she loves will boost her comfort level. Ezra made do with Jonah's hand-me-down Winnie the Pooh backpack, but he did get to choose his own lunch box.

"Look! There's Baxter from Little Guppies!"

Do you like walking into parties where you don't know a soul? Me neither. Try to connect with parents of future classmates. Seeing a friendly face on the first day will be a boon for everyone.

"Ariel Would Love Preschool, Especially If It Was Underwater."

Does she love Violet from *The Incredibles*? Ask her to imagine what Violet would do on her first day of preschool. Would she be shy? Would she remember that she has superpowers and could put a force field around her if she was scared? See if your daughter wants to pretend she is Violet on the first day (or week). Or Dora, Princess Jasmine, Ariel, or anyone else who has shown bravery in her favorite stories and movies. That might give her the extra boldness she needs.

Create Rituals

Four hugs for each year he's blown out candles, Eskimo kisses, a secret handshake, a high five—a fun, sweet little tradition as you're parting will make the good-bye easier on both of you.

Don't Just Vaporize

Always tell your child that you are leaving, as tempting as it is to sneak out just as your little one has found someone she knows or something that has caught her interest. You may think it would be easier not to tell her, but it's only easier for you. Do prepare her. "Mom's going to look at this artwork for a few minutes, and then it's time for me to go." Don't hover, and don't tear up! OK, so you can tear up, but remember, pretend you're allergic to the classroom hamster, and don't let on that your sniffles are the result of gut-wrenching, child-abandoning anguish. Not such an actress? Say bye and make a mad dash for the car. That's what I always do, and I haven't been caught yet.

FUN THINGS

Mommalies: Sayings Our Mothers Hurled at Us That We Now Hurl at Our Youngsters

If you sit too close to the TV, you'll go blind. "That is *so* not true," they'll reply when they get to the age where they don't buy those sayings anymore. And they would be *so* right. Why do we as moms feel so uncomfortable with the sight of our rug spuds' little faces pasted to the tube? Maybe we feel guilty about them watching too much TV, or maybe it just looks like it hurts their eyes, even if it doesn't. It's like Grandma saying, "Put a sweater on—you're making me cold." It's all subjective, so we perpetuate the myth to the next generation.

Don't make me stop this car. Like you're gonna stop the car while cruising a shoulderless interstate, semitrucks whizzing by at eighty-five miles per hour. But they don't know that! I think they must really wonder, *What would happen if Mom and Dad stopped the car? Would we be strapped to the top, like the deer Uncle Marty got last hunting season? Would we have to walk home? Could the police become involved?* With possibilities this ominous, it's no wonder this threat works so well. Don't overuse it, though, because at some point their pint-sized psyches are going to figure out you have never brought the vehicle to a complete stop after issuing this fulmination, so it is likely you never will.

Oh, you don't have to get me anything for Mother's Day. Uh-huh. The kids don't, of course. They can present you with a Popsicle stick frame or a Fruit Loop rendering of a flower, and you'll be thrilled. Jonah's preschool portrait of Mom looking like a scarecrow with frog eyes is among my prized possessions. But Daddy? Now *he* has to get you something for Mother's Day. Flowers, jewelry—perhaps in a setting featuring one or all of your children's birthstones—these are both good. (When you utter the above sentence, very dramatically emphasize the word "you." This way your main man cannot mistake the meaning of this sentence or assume he falls under the jurisdiction of "you.")

Don't cry over spilled milk. Spilled chocolate milk or grape juice—now that you can cry about.

You're not leaving the house dressed like that. Oy vey. That little ensemble miss diva has chosen—bathing suit over leotard, under a leopard-print poncho, with green rubber boots—is hurting your eyes. Mr. Blackwell would never approve, but then again, he never had a four-year-old fashionista in the house.

Turn down that music this instant! OK, so it's not the Duran Duran or Def Leppard you listened to as a teenager, but that Wiggles CD is making you want to run down the street screaming.

9

"WHACK THE PIÑATA, NOT THE CAKE!"

Throwing a smashing birthday bash

YOU ALL KNOW by now that I am the furthest thing from a domestic goddess. The only "home art" I have any skill in seems to be decorating. Cleaning? Cooking? Laundry? Um . . . I'll do it later. However, my parents, fastidious creatures that they are, seem to enjoy cleaning my home when they come to visit twice a year, so I say, "Have at it, folks! Don't have too much fun with that bleach pen, now!" Hey, whatever floats their boats.

Seeing as I am almost entirely right-brained, a domestic endeavor has to somehow capture my fancy, spark my imagination, and get those creative juices flowing. That's why decorating is right up my alley. Choosing a new shower curtain, then, is grounds for giddiness, and flipping through the new Pottery Barn catalog gives me goose bumps. Selecting paint colors for the baby's nursery? I could just cry with joy.

Happily, at least one mothering enterprise—besides naming the children and decorating their rooms—involves color, shimmer, whimsy, and creation: I'm talking birthday parties, friend! I love every celebratory step, from having a little confab with the birthday child about this year's theme (I am over-the-top on themes) to invitations, favors, and—be still my heart—concocting the pièce de résistance, the cake.

Yes, the laundry can pile to the ceiling, and the dust bunnies procreate like, well, bunnies, but my children will have a fab-oo cake for their birthdays. Now, don't be deceived—I'm not one of those moms who hires a mariachi band or a clown at her child's fete. "Simple" is still the buzzword, even though the Martha mind-set does kind of possess me for a short time leading up to the big day. One time we did contemplate cobbling together a kind of ad hoc petting zoo from our menagerie and that of close neighbors. We had a dog, a couple of cats, a snail, the kindergarten gerbil billeted with us for the summer, and Goldfarb the goldfish, not pet-able but always viewable. Plus, Brooklyn down the street had a boa constrictor and a rat that had just had babies. Well, maybe a petting zoo wasn't such a great idea after all. The whole idea of a big snake kind of stopped me in my tracks.

So no petting zoo, but we still usually manage to throw a pretty cool wingding for our boys—simple yet big fun, and always tuned in to what it is they are crazy about that particular year. And that, my party-phobic pals, is the key to a grand-slam *par-tay* the offspring will remember forever.

It'll Be a Party to Remember

"Your child's birthday doesn't have to be a major undertaking. It also doesn't have to impress everyone you know or make your child cry before it's finished," says Shelly Radic, author of *The Birthday Book*. "Instead, at the end of your child's birthday, he or she should know without a doubt that [he or] she is a one-of-a-kind, uniquely created individual, truly special and dearly loved."[1]

Make the Birthday Boy Co-chair

Erika Stremler Pott enlisted the help of her mom, mother-in-law, sister-in-law, and friend for her son Max's birthday party when he turned four and a half. Max was born in December, so he and his parents decided on a half birthday. "It was Max's idea to have a party, and it was his idea to have it in the summer," says Pott. Max's party included tie-dying T-shirts, a piñata, face painting (Dad did the work), and a fish pond. They created dirt cupcakes (chocolate cake, crushed Oreos, and gummy worms) and put the ice cream in a giant flowerpot. "Max was in on every idea for the party," says his mom.[2]

Thumping Good Themes

In the preplanning, hook into your child's current fixations, or at least try to come up with a theme the birthday guest of honor would enjoy. Our biggest successes were Jonah's four-year-old camping party and Ezra's three-year-old horse-themed gala. At the camping bash, we rented out the gym of our church and actually pitched a tent inside (it

111

was December). We decorated moose cookies and played games around the "campfire." The cake, another "campfire," was an amazingly simple concoction, although it looked like I had slaved hours over it. (The secret was the crushed Jolly Rancher candies that I melted, solidified, and broke into shards for "fire." A snap and so slick looking.) The reason we celebrated camping was that the previous summer Jonah had gone camping with his dad and loved our new tent so much he wanted to take naps inside when it was pitched in our yard.

When Ezra turned three, he was at the height of his enthusiasm for all things horsey. In every photo we have of our second son during this time, he is holding at least one plastic horse. Grandpa was beside himself; finally the cowboy gene showed up in someone! So it was a no-brainer to do a horse theme, complete with "pin the tail on the stallion," goody bags tied in bandanas, and a horse-head cake from a *Family Fun* Internet recipe.

Other Awesome Motifs

Kelly threw a ladybug party for her daughter's third birthday. She sent out five packaged ladybug cards (following up with a phone call to make sure at least three guests could come), held a plastic ladybug hunt in the backyard, and served ladybug cupcakes bought at the bakery. No fuss for Kelly—the total cost was under thirty-five dollars, and the payoff was a cozy, intimate party her daughter loved.

A Hawaiian luau with leis, a tropical dress code, and fun, fruity drinks with umbrellas in them warm up a wintry birthday. Hula hoops make apropos favors! Or why not have a snowman party? We've done it, and nothing could be simpler or cuter than snowman cake, invites, and crafts. The trickiest part was coaxing a couple of cold-hating partygoers to join us outside to build and decorate the snowman.

Rockets, dinosaurs, and bulldozers are all nifty notions for boy parties too. Jonah's shark party, tied to his obsession with the great white when he turned five and a half, was announced with invites festooned with shark stickers on underwater scrapbook paper. The "cake" was actually blue Jell-O with gummy sharks, set in a springform pan and iced with whipped cream. The kids went nuts over those creepy slabs of Jell-O, I'm happy to say!

Keep It Small for Now

The rule of thumb we obey is to invite one little guest for every year of the child's life, plus one more if three or four seems like too few kids (or your sister has triplets). We hosted nine kids at a movie for Jonah's four-and-a-half birthday party, and of course it was too many. Luckily, Grandma helped and little brother Ez was home with a babysitter. Still, if I had it to do over, I'd stick with five kids.

Jen T. can also speak from experience about guest overload:

Our daughter Gabbi turned three this year, and we had a huge party two weeks after our second daughter, Lexi, was born. It turned out to be almost sixty people at our house! It was a great success and fun. But it would have been more relaxing to have it a little smaller. I heard, and I think it's a good idea, to match the number of friends invited to the age your child is turning. Therefore, we were a little off and should have had . . . fifty-seven people fewer!

Christy concurs: "Don't ever invite eight kids and let their moms come with younger siblings!" she says. "I ended up with eight three-year-olds, eight moms, and seven toddlers for Grace's birthday. It was a mess! It took me an hour and a half just to put all the toys away!"

Icing Issues

Kim says,

Birthday parties in my husband's family are a big deal and an every-year affair. On my side of the family, we had a big party on special birthdays like five and ten, but for the in-between years we usually invited one or two friends or just celebrated with our own family. So it's been work to compete with what his family expects, but it's also been fun.

On Elana's first birthday I had grand plans to make this amazing cake. She liked rabbits, so I was going to make a bunny cake. The cutout turned out well, but when it came time to do the frosting, well, I was running a little short on time. The frosting that I had made from scratch turned out to be too runny, and nothing I did to thicken it seemed to work, so it kind of ran off the cake and puddled on the sides. The decorating tools didn't seem to work as the frosting was too thick—or maybe I just didn't know how to make it properly. Suffice it to say, I couldn't get the frosting to come out in nice, smooth lines. Anyway, my daughter ended up with a bunny cake that didn't have much of a face, and the words "Happy 1st birthday" were all squiggly. For subsequent birthday parties, I've learned to plan ahead, to get ideas in plenty of time online or in parenting magazines, and—this is key—to buy store-bought frosting instead of making my own!

The Goody Bag Is Alive and Well

I know one mom who refuses to give goody bags at her child's birthdays. Her beef? "Those things are just full of cheap junk anyway that will break within two days!" I say, c'mon, what modern child doesn't adore a trip to the dollar store, which is teeming with cheap, junky, breakable, irresistible trinkets? You can hire cast members from *The Lion King* to serenade your party guests, but if they go home empty-handed, they ain't happy campers. Their loot can even be food. For Jonah's third birthday—his first with friends—I chose a whale theme for him because, after all, his name is Jonah. His four little guests trotted home that day toting plastic baggies filled with blue Jell-O and brightly colored gummy fish. Sometimes a goody bag can be as simple as one item for each child that is ideally tied into the party's theme. For our snowman party, I found two-dollar fizzy "snowballs" that effervesce in the tub. One mom actually sent me a thank-you note—*for a party favor*—because her son was so psyched about that fizzy snowball!

Hit the dollar store and you'll hit pay dirt on goody bag fillers. Once I even found some brightly colored mini trash cans—four for a dollar—that I used as my bags.

Sidewalk chalk, Play-Doh containers (little ones are supercheap), stickers, rubber bugs, snakes, dinosaurs, metal cars, doll accessories, bubbles—the list of possibilities will make your child's friends say, "Oh, goody." (I couldn't resist!)

More Smashing Bash Ideas from the Preschool Panel

Kim: I've made cookie dough and let the kids create their own cookies, and that is a big hit. (Refrigerated, slice-and-bake dough is perfect for this. Add tubes of colorful gel icing, edible markers, mini rolling pins, and cookie cutters and you have an easy, super-fun activity both boys and girls will love.)

Ann: My best birthday party idea comes from my childhood. My mom (who is a high school teacher) used to take a page of my favorite coloring book or character of the year and have her students do a huge mural using an opaque projector. These murals were a great decoration and photo backdrop for my parties!

Brenna: My best birthday idea for three- to five-year-olds: take them to the children's museum, where there are nonstop activities available and fun, fun, fun. Add a cake—and voilà! You've got an instant party and you don't have to clean up afterward. (How about the botanical gardens, a nature center, a gymnastics gym for a tumbling party, or a gym for floor hockey, basketball, or parachute games?)

Cheryl's Top Eight List for Savvy Celebrations

1. However many games you think you'll need, double it.
2. Give prizes to all kids, especially young ones, for all games—it doesn't have to be fabulous, but it needs to be something.

3. Here's a good outside or summer game: buy a big bag (lots of pieces) of wrapped, nonmelting candy. Hide it all over the yard in relatively easy-to-find places. Give all the kids a paper bag with their name on it and have them find the candy. This works well as the first game of the day to burn off energy.
4. Never give loud toys (whistles, kazoos) or weapons (squirt guns, slingshots) as prizes.
5. Don't open up (unpackage) all the new toys at the party—something always gets lost or broken.
6. Remind your birthday child before the party that he or she is the host—therefore he or she needs to share, use best manners, be kind, open cards first, and so on.
7. Take a picture of all the kids together before the party gets going. It's the only time they won't be a blur!
8. Thank-you notes to your child's friends should be mandatory. You can take a picture of the birthday child with each friend and use it as a thank-you postcard.

Are Thank-You Cards Really Mandatory?

If there's one thing my mother drilled into me, it's that thank-you cards are a great idea, if not a must. I don't get them out for every occasion, unfortunately. After Christmas, I've pretty much given up, although I have every intention of reviving that social nicety—next Christmas! But I do try to guide the thank-you note process following my sons' birthday parties. They're a courtly, kindly tradition from a courtlier, kindlier time, and having to write them teaches kids that we should actually express our gratitude for presents we've received. Up until Jonah could write his own, I admit

More Ways to Domesticate Your Little Chore Kids

Folding laundry. Oh, goody—matching games! Matching socks is a good way to get started. You don't like this job anyway, and it can occupy your junior sock matcher for quite some time. Separate the dark colors from the light ones, then see if he can match up the pairs. Later, he can sort the clothes by category—shirts here, pants there—and even put his own clothes in his dresser drawers.

Dusting. It takes only a small investment to purchase a feather duster, and kids love them—they tickle, they're funny, and they work. Designate the areas that need cleaning and any that are off-limits. Since the feather duster allows your child to extend his reach, make sure he knows what not to touch. Remove Aunt Bertha's Hummel figurine collection and let the dusting whiz go for it.

Sweeping and vacuuming. Pass the vacuuming to your five-year-old? Well, maybe not quite yet. But do let her run the carpet sweeper over the rug, especially if she's made a mess herself that needs cleaning up. It's good to instill the idea that mom's not the maid and to let those untidy little guys and girls take some age-appropriate ownership of their own messes. (Hint: "Redo" if you must when the child is asleep. That way you won't undermine her confidence in her ability to clean up!)

I composed the notes for him, only requiring that he sign his name in some fashion. A better idea is to have young ones draw a picture of the present, or create some kind of picture, and then also "sign" their names. (A three-year-old can get by with scrawling an "E" or "Z," whatever the first letter of his name is.)

This year for Ezra's thank-you notes, I grabbed a cute little make-your-own-card kit (less than three dollars at Target) with premade cards and envelopes, glue, glitter, stickers, and scads of little foam shapes. They were perfect and truly bore the unique stamp of their creator! If you do write a little note, don't get nervous if you've lost your list of who gave what to whom. And you don't really have to write an essay about the many uses for the item you and your child have found. "Many thanks to you, Emma, for the unique and fascinating soap sculpture, which we use as a . . . one-of–a-kind paperweight." In these sticky social scenarios, just express thanks for coming and sharing in the fun of the day.

FUN THINGS

How to Throw a Birthday Bash for a Three-Year-Old

1. A month before the big day, contemplate how many of your child's amigos should be invited to his party. Disregarding the "one child per year of age" rule, you choose to invite the entire Sunday school class—nine little ones—thinking there's a snowball's chance in Florida that all of them will RSVP.

2. Panic when you field nine phone calls, all from parents RSVP-ing to your child's party.

3. Fret over the fact that "Tessa the Terrible" is coming, and here you thought her family went to Myrtle Beach every single spring break.

4. Mull over a theme for the party. Bob the Builder? Too commercial, you think. Dora the Explorer? Too girlie, even though seven out of nine party guests are girls. Dinosaurs? Perhaps too scary, in light of your child's new fear of absolutely everything.

5. Ask your husband what theme he thinks the party should be. "Theme?" he says, completely flummoxed. "Why does there have to be a theme?" Realize he's the wrong person to ask.

6. Choose a bunny motif, figuring boys and girls both love bunnies, and they're not too scary, and hey—how cute is this theme going to be?

7. Take a deep breath when your husband comments that the bunny theme isn't really a guy's thing. State as nicely as you can that Howie Jr. is a *little boy*, not a *guy*, for heaven's sake! And it is close to Easter, after all.

8. Proceed with the bunny theme, going so far as to borrow a couple of darling little baby rabbits from a neighbor and— the pièce de résistance—a baby chick from the preschool class. The kids in the class are all on spring break and won't miss it.

9. Order a bunny cake from the local bakery with the words "Happy third birthday, Howie" to appear under a precious woodland rabbit made of buttercream icing.

10. Label the goody bags, laboring for some time over whether the correct spelling is Mykayla, Mikaelah, or Michaela.

11. On the day of the party, check on the chick and see that overnight the critter has turned into a gnarly looking chicken, one that seems to poop seventeen times a day.

12. Have a cow when your husband brings home the cake with a German shepherd on it and the words "Happy thirtieth birthday, Humvee." Decide it's too late for a new cake but vow to never use that bakery again. Yeah, that'll teach 'em.

13. Greet Tessa and her mother at the door, and wince when the birthday boy says, "What's she doin' here? I don' *wike* her!"

14. Grit your teeth when Tessa's alpha mommy says smugly, "Who's Humvee?"

15. As the next hour and a half proceeds, oversee party games, cake distribution, the smashing of the bunny piñata, and the potty action of ten preschoolers.

16. Grasp that at least one or two of the party guests are not really potty trained, per se.

17. Comfort nine children as they stand in a corner crying because Tessa let the chicken out and it scared them.

18. Wipe chicken poop off everyone's feet.

19. Wince when Howie opens up a toy from a show he's not allowed to watch and then proceeds to tell the gift giver, "This is naughty to play with, so here—I don't want it."

20. Slump in a chair with relief when the last guest leaves, vowing to swear off bakeries, bunnies, and chickens forevermore—or at least until Howie turns four.

10

Extreme Granny Makeover

Finessing those annoying little grandparent issues

KELLY'S MOM IS always telling her she'll ruin little Jadon if she doesn't potty train him before his baby sister arrives. Krista's mother-in-law constantly drops by unannounced to see her "darling boy" and then proceeds to take over his care and feeding—in Krista's house! Pam's father-in-law is appalled at the "loosey-goosey" way Pam and Brad discipline their son, and he's not afraid to tell them so, sometimes in front of little Brody.

These are true stories, unfortunately, each one told to me as I travel around speaking at moms groups. I never fail to be amazed at the angst caused by differences in opinion between young parents and their one-generation-older parents. To be honest, I can't completely relate. My parents and in-laws are pretty hands-off when it comes to how I raise my kids. Oh, I've gotten comments here and there that have bugged me at least a little. My dad thinks it's slapdash indeed when we occasionally eat a meal in front of the TV. Doyle's dad has this sort of John Wayne mentality that men of all ages shouldn't wear shorts or sandals, and he has mentioned this more than once. And one of the grandmas thinks the kids are somewhat lacking in table manners. Although that's not the way she puts it, I can clearly read between the lines.

But I've never experienced the outright rancor, competitiveness, and deep hurt between the two generations that so many young couples have felt. Whether your issues with the grandparents of your kids are just annoying, or worse, here's a guide to tackling the most common problems our generation of moms faces. I'm calling the solutions "Extreme Granny Makeover," but "Granny" in this case represents Gramps too.

Granny Just Does Things Differently

Few mothers and daughters do their job of mothering in exactly the same way, so there's bound to be a little bit of misunderstanding, if not friction. In some ways, every family is a different culture, so when you marry into your husband's family, it can be like marrying into a new civilization, with varied "laws" and ways of doing things.

Kim truly married into a whole new world when she wed Sam from Nigeria. Like in any other daughter-in-law/parents-in-law relationship, there's been some need for give-and-take:

For me, I guess the touchiest stuff in our relationship comes from the difference in my culture and my husband's. Respect is a big thing in my husband's culture—right down to using titles for anyone that's even a few years older than you. It's expected that you call so-and-so Aunt or Uncle even though they aren't related, just so you aren't calling them by their first name. Trying to emphasize this extreme to my kids is going to be difficult growing up in the States. I worry that I may be criticized by his family for how my kids turn out. For now, I know in my heart that they are kind and polite for their ages—Elana already says her pleases and thank-yous at appropriate times, for example. Although we do plan to spend time in Africa as well as here, I don't know quite how the girls will be affected by all of it. My hope is that they'll take the best of both cultures and blend it into something great.

Bottom line: Different generation, different personalities, and different backgrounds shape you, your parents, and your in-laws, so Granny may well think you're doing things wrong because you're not doing things her way.

Extreme Granny makeover: Next time your mother-in-law sniffs that her little Bobby never ate "that fast-food junk," try not to get defensive. Hard, I know. Try to use a light touch to disarm her ("Then I wonder why he's so chunky, because it sure isn't my home cooking!"), and show her you understand at least partially where she's coming from. "I know fast food was probably worse in those days than it is now. These days they have fruit juice, milk, and applesauce on the menu for kids. We usually get the chicken strips and some apple juice when we go through the drive-through, and it's such a treat for Cate." Leave it at that, because less is more here. Try to keep in mind that she also didn't drive much when your husband was small, on account of their having one car. Her lifestyle was completely different than your mobile, out-and-about days with your little ones. She just doesn't get it.

Granny Takes Charge

This one's a doozy! Granny and Gramps act as if they, not you and your husband, are the parents. They scold your preschooler in front of you; they worry about what he wears, what he watches on television, and what time he goes to bed; and they expect to spend massive amounts of time with their grandchild. Yikes!

In the next section, you'll read about Lindsay and her "perfect" mother-in-law, who also likes to take over with the grandkids whenever possible. "Now that all her kids are gone and having their own families, she still wants to have that mothering role," says Lindsay. "She tends to tell us how to parent every chance she gets. You can feel her kick into parent mode as soon as we walk in the door." Lindsay has hit on a great insight here: Granny yearns to be back in the role that defined her life, so she can't stop telling her kids how to run their lives. Essentially, she doesn't show her son and daughter-in-law the respect they deserve.

Two panel moms commented on how their kiddies' grandparents had a habit of interfering with naps (that alone is grounds for a restraining order!). "I am a scheduler," says Amy. "What I mean is I have routines for my children. My mother and in-laws go by the demand-care system. They go by what they perceive my children to need. For example, if

Ashley doesn't appear tired, they might not give her a nap. But I rarely let her skip her nap."

Christy has a similar problem. "Putting the kids down for naps when grandparents are around is always hard because they don't understand that the kids need the naps; they just want to see their grandchildren." Subtext: "We know better than you when your child needs a nap."

One severe case of take-charge granny is Krista's mother-in-law. "It's like she thinks I'm a moron or something!" she vented. "Scott's mom doesn't seem to recognize boundaries in our home. She'll drop by unannounced with lunch for her precious grandson—none for me, of course! She'll even say, 'Time for your nap, sweets,' when it's time for her to leave, although he just got up from a nap when she came."

Bottom line: Who's in charge here? That's the question of the hour.

Extreme Granny makeover: Remind yourself you're in charge—you and your husband—not Granny. It's your household, your rules, your philosophy of naps. Just do things your way, be confident in your parenting choices, and enforce boundaries. For example, Krista could ask Scott to deal with his mother: "Mom, thanks so much for all the help and stuff, but we have our own way of doing things. How about this: when you take Scottie Junior on Mondays, your rules apply, and the rest of the week, our rules apply." Sounds like Scott's mom needs to get a life of her own too.

Take-charge grandparents are basically well meaning—they really think they can help by doing things their way—but their choleric ways undermine your confidence and authority as a parent. Maybe they could scratch that itch with more one-on-one time with the grandkids. If you could use a break (and who couldn't?), take advantage of their turbo grandparenting urges and drop off your kids for a few hours a week. If they felt more secure in their bond with the kids, maybe they would back off a little when you're around.

Granny Is "Perfect"

Now, my mother-in-law is a domestic queen who cooks and cleans circles around me, but she never rubs it in my face, which is one reason we get along so well. Lindsay's MIL, in sharp contrast, seems to enjoy taking advantage of her superiority in the home arts a little too much.

> I think part of what creates tension between Sue and me is the fact that she's spent the last thirty years being a "super-mom." We're talking candlelight dinners, gourmet school lunches (even love notes every day on their napkins), home-made cookies after school each day, and—get this—she heats everyone's plates before every meal.
>
> Not only do I find it hard not to compare myself to the supermom my husband grew up with, but I also struggle with the fact that she comes across as a "super-Christian." She often talks about how she spends two to three hours each morning praising and praying. I have never heard her apologize (her husband, Gerry, says she hasn't in thirty-five years of marriage), and she apparently doesn't struggle with many sins either. Sue often says she doesn't struggle with jealousy or having her feelings hurt, for example. It seems to me that she thinks she's reached the point of perfection.

Bottom line: Granny's all that and a bag of homemade cookies. How can her daughter-in-law ever hope to measure up?

Extreme Granny makeover: That's just it. No one will ever measure up to Sue, who sees herself as She Who Will Be Revered. For some reason, she has to maintain an image of "perfection," which, if I were a shrink, would lead me to believe things are not as perfect as they seem. And this bit about never saying she's sorry in thirty-five years of marriage? That's just scary. I think Granny should pray for some humility while she's on her knees for three hours a day!

Lindsay's got to resolve in her mind that Granny will never change, and that's Granny's problem. She will never live up to this plate-heating control nut. Clearly Granny's got some issues, but Lindsay cannot get hooked into this unspoken competition thing. She's got to let it go and not let her relationship with her mother-in-law become toxic. So Granny's perfect? Good for Granny. You be the best mom you can, as Lindsay is seeking to do. "I'm trying to choose to love her when she says controlling and insensitive comments," says Lindsay. "I'm trying to remain positive when she frustrates me to no end. I know I need to make the choice for my family's sake."

Granny's from the Old School

Here we are, ladies, at the crux of many generational disputes: there are old school and new school ways of doing things, and sometimes the differences are quite noticeable! "I notice this difference in opinions probably more with my own mother than I do with my mother-in-law," says Jen T. "My pediatrician seems to say different things than my mother's pediatrician told her thirty years ago. For instance, I will have my baby dressed in an outfit, drop her off at my mom's, and come home after running errands to find a baby suffocating under a bunch of clothes. My mom will have put on tights under the outfit and added a sweater. 'To keep her warm, honey!' she will say."

When Granny's from the old school, she'll reject new parenting information and practices. Did she work a part-time job outside the home when you were little? Nooo. Did she place a great deal of value on her and your dad "coparenting" you and your siblings? No, that would have smacked of "women's lib." She spanked you when you had a tantrum and feels you're coddling little Lucy when you help her work through her out-of-control emotions. You cleaned your plate—no ifs, ands, or buts—and she's horrified you occasionally let your daughter go to bed slightly hungry to teach her a lesson. And if Granny says "Look how you turned out!" one more time, you'll scream.

Even the most close-knit mothers and daughters must agree to disagree on these old school/new school matters. "We don't have major disputes; however, my mom and I disagree about the urgency of training Josephine to quit sucking her thumb," says Mary Jo. "I waited until after Louisa's birth so as not to 'traumatize' her while a new little one was on the way and about to be arriving in her home."

Bottom line: That was then, this is now, and therein lies the rub.

Extreme Granny makeover: Get inside Granny's head a little bit and you may develop some understanding of where she's coming from. "Because [grandparents] have already raised all their children, they probably see themselves as parenting experts and just assume you're going to welcome all their parenting advice," says Susan Newman, Ph.D. "Becoming grandparents may also make them feel a bit old—an uncomfortable feeling that's exacerbated whenever you explain to them that they're not up-to-date on important aspects of child rearing."[1]

Can you imagine how you'd feel, thirty years from now, if the American Academy of Pediatrics suddenly reversed their official stances on some big issues? If young mothers were told to let their babies sleep on their tummies again and to quit breast-feeding because formula will "fatten them up" better? You would be dumbfounded! It's not hard to understand why our mothers are at least a little confused and possibly defensive. "You mean to tell me all of those rules I followed when I was raising you are no longer valid?"

I have used the response, "Isn't it crazy the way things change?" It helps take the edge off when you imply the changes are out of both your hands, and what can you do but follow your doctor's orders? Do invoke your doctor whenever you can. Make him or her the bad guy. I've been quoting Dr. Kevin Leman on issues of discipline—"Leman says we've got to make reality the teacher in these situations"—and that seems to mollify any critics in the crowd. Cut out pertinent articles that support your case too. That way Granny won't think you've made these wacky things up just to drive her crazy.

Granny's Always Got a Jab

"Sandy's grandson is already reading words like 'cat' and 'dog,'" your mother-in-law remarks once over Sunday lunch. "But of course his mother works so much with him that it's to be expected."

Subtext: you're not drilling in enough phonics or zipping through enough flashcards with her precious grandson. ("That's great that Sandy's daughter makes time for that sort of thing," you want to say. "I'm always too busy watching soaps and eating bonbons!")

Does it seem like your parents or in-laws always throw a little zinger at you, in subtle and not-so-subtle ways? Criticisms, even implied ones, can hurt like crazy. Nothing gets a mother's hackles up like someone calling her skills less than stellar. Was Bailey potty trained at three years and nine months? You likely heard about it in a thousand backhanded comments. Does Mia cling to your leg at family gatherings? It's because you "baby" her too much, of course. Are your twin boys caught jumping on Granny's new sofa "like a bunch of wild animals"? Mom has no control—*obviously.*

Ouch. Jabs from the oldsters can make you feel inadequate like nothing else. "It seems like as soon as you have children, your parents and in-laws see it as a license to provide unsolicited advice," says Jodi. "I just listen with an open mind. I tell myself they are not living under our roof, so they really don't know the whole picture. Sometimes I try to look for an itsy, tiny kernel of truth in the advice and then call some of my best girlfriends for their input."

Bottom line: Little snide remarks and jabs pile up, and after a while they can threaten your relationship with your parents or in-laws. It's time for tough love.

Extreme Granny makeover: Granny's got to put a sock in it, or else. You or your husband, whoever is the calmer party, needs to call her on it as tactfully as possible. "Mom, we love you, and the kids adore you, but it does undermine our job as parents when you make those kinds of comments."

"What kinds of comments?" she may ask, completely flummoxed. Have a couple of examples ready to go. "You know, when you said Harry's head wouldn't be so flat if we had put him to sleep on his stomach when he was smaller. That kind of thing." She may not even be aware of how critical she can come across. "It may be just us feeling touchy as new parents, but we have been feeling kind of judged lately. We know you mean well, but could you try to be more positive in your remarks? That would make us feel really supported as we raise Harry."

Don't Forget . . .

You need your parents and in-laws in your life, so it's worth the effort to patch up any tears in the relationship. Remember, some people would give anything to have their parents back or to have doting grandparents in their children's lives. It may not be easy to mend fences, or to just get along, but the benefits for your whole family will be rich, if not always tangible.

To end on a positive note, here are a couple of rave reviews from Cheryl about her parents and in-laws:

I have the most wonderful, serene mother-in-law in the whole world. My in-laws are very different from me, but they are a huge blessing to all of us. They are safety and security and love.

My mom is a totally on-the-floor, just-as-goofy-as-the-kids kind of grandma. She always treats kids as real people with important things to say. She believes in chocolate chip cookies for breakfast. She's still a child at heart, fun to be with, quick to laugh, and full of love.

Instill Their Green Ethic Now

Find new uses. Rather than chucking toilet paper rolls, papers written on one side, baby wipe boxes, fabric, and paper scraps, use them for crafts. You don't have to do a craft with the item right that minute, but save it in a "craft box" for a rainy day.

Reuse food. Preschool teachers are showing kids how to compost. Why not try it at home? Put fruit and vegetable scraps, eggshells, and a few dead leaves from outside in a composting container, and in no time the materials will turn to soil. Then use the composted soil and grow pretty flowers with your child.

Teach them about the recycle box. With your child watching, separate the garbage from the items that can be placed in the recycle box. Explain how they can be used again when they are recycled.

My dad is getting a second chance with grandparenting, and he's generally doing a better job than with parenting. He's been a real man in a man's world for a long time, but he's starting to figure out what a blessing children are, how quickly they grow up, and that they can really be a lot of fun to be with. He's trying to pass on his passion for the outdoors and hunting to Nathanael, and he is bemused by and doing his best to understand the girlie-girl world Adrielle loves. These two beautiful Korean children have done more for racial reconciliation in my father's life than all the civil rights leaders ever have. He's discovered unconditional love.

FUN THINGS

Overheard at Preschool, Part 3

Anthony: "My mom said I have to try something ten times before I will like it. But I think only eight times."

Miss Susan: "What does 'romantic music' mean?"
Jordan: "It's dancing, and you get your whole body out."

Noah: "People in Africa walk around with roofs on their heads, and wherever they stop, that's where their house is."

Paige: "My mom can make spoiled water!"

Delaney: "When I play house, I like to be the mom 'cuz moms get to be the boss."

Mirabella: "Miss Susan, why are you in the naughty chair?"

Scottie: "I am eating two Starbucks [Starburst]!"

Miss Jessie: "Adios, muchachos!"
Thomas: "Adios, tomatoes!"

Miss Susan: "I think we should go to the Lord in prayer. What do you think?"

Morgan: "I think we should go to Indiana!"

Ezra: "I am *definitely* not a screwball!"

11

"CAN WE TALK?"

Making and keeping mommy pals

WHEN YOUR LITTLE guy renders his sister's Barbies headless, asks your neighbor why she's "sooo fat," or refuses to eat anything green or orange—who ya gonna call? Your mommy friends! Mothering is intense, but it's made much more doable and even enjoyable when the ups and downs can be shared with our buddies.

I would venture to say I wouldn't make it very far as a mom if I didn't have some rock-solid pals around to help carry the load, emotionally at least. And by "around" I mean accessible by phone or email. My forebears on my mother's side were Red River Valley pioneers—a sod house and the whole nine (thousand) yards of prairie. I've reflected more than once that had I been my great-great-grandma, stuck in the middle of nowhere, only seeing friends every week or so at church, I would have gone stark, raving mad.

Thankfully, I have access to the women who have made me not only a better person but a more effective, loving mom too.

Some of you reading this are in a place like my new friend Kimberley—possibly new to town and lonely, isolated, and aching for the kinship and laughter friends share. When I speak to moms groups and at conferences, I am amazed at hearing the same story over and over: "It's just me and my kids in the house, and I don't really have any friends right now."

I just feel sore inside for these young women, and I remember with a twinge of pain the times I have spent hungry for the understanding, grace, and encouragement only girlfriends can provide.

We moms need each other more than ever while in the trenches of this giving, sacrificial, draining endeavor. We need the bolstering of someone understanding when our three-year-old has flushed our watch down the toilet. We need a hand to hold when our child is faced with medical problems. We need to laugh—somehow—when our son manages to set off the sprinkler in the car (see Cheryl's story on page 151). We need our friends!

Making New Friends

I had a single friend once who would always say she was "in between" boyfriends at the moment, which always kind of made me wonder why she never seemed to be just "in" a relationship with a guy. You too might feel like you're "in between" friends right now. Your college friends are all far away, and your single friends don't have a clue about potty training or teething or tantrums. And those other young moms at your church or in your neighborhood? They seem pretty cool, but how do you make the leap from friendly acquaintance to bona fide pal?

I'm so glad you asked! The art of making real friends out of potential friends is one skill that will stand you in good stead over and over as you parent your little guys and girls. Here, then, are some jumping-off points for you to make that all-important leap.

Scout Out Support Groups

If you're not enrolled already, scout out local MOPS groups and other mothering support-type groups. There's nothing like them for gathering like-minded chicks together for fun, food, and—the best part—two hours of freedom from those children you adore. "I love MOPS because I now feel that I'm not the only one who loses her patience with her kids once in a while," says Kim. "I've also gotten some great advice on potty training, the lima bean snack [page 57], and so much more." Kim herself is a freelance photographer who specializes in taking wonderful pictures of kids, so she's been able to share her knowledge of cameras and angles with all the snap-happy moms in her group. Don't have a mom group in your area? Start one! Invite a few of those fellow moms you know but don't *know* over for some cookies and a play date. See if they'd like to host next time, and build from there. It takes a pinch of boldness to be the one to reach out first, but the rewards can be fantastic.

Find Moms Who Groove on the Same Hobbies

Yes, you have child rearing in common with other moms, but that doesn't mean you will automatically have that "spark" that kindred spirits always have, so keep other fun options in mind. Like to read? A book club is fabulous, and it gives you an excuse to delve into some juicy, provocative, buzz-worthy tomes. Scrapbooking is a glove-fit for moms who love to cut, paste, and color (because we miss kindergarten—at least, I do!). Listen to Mary talk about her nifty club:

> Every other month, I meet with a group of seven friends for Cooking Light Night. They take turns hosting and place one person in charge of planning the menu and assigning a dish to each person in the group. Those assigned dishes familiarize themselves with the recipe, bring the necessary ingredients, and show how the recipe is prepared when their turn comes during our cooking. The best part of the evening is sitting down to eat the meal we've just prepared together and enjoying the fellowship that occurs.[1]

Cut the Alpha Mommy Act and Be Yourself

This is the single most important ingredient in making new friends—well, besides basic friendliness. You must be open about your mommy *stuff*, about what's really going on beneath the cute soccer mom duds. In other words, you can't prance around pretending all is superfabulous in your life at home with your kids. (This doesn't mean blabbing on and on about your mother-in-law's colonoscopy to someone you've just met. Use your noodle, girls.) What bonds us as friends is the opportunity to lift each other up when we are discouraged, downtrodden, or lacking direction. But we don't get that opportunity to give or receive grace and guidance if we maintain the alpha mommy façade. Take that chance to open up about some kid issue that's been nagging at you. "Karis is so belligerent these days. She never wants to wear anything I've chosen for her, and she used to be so compliant about everything!" Or throw out a question at your next mommy-child play date: "Hey, I was wondering about how Tom and I could get out more without the kids. Do you guys have a date night?" Just asking for advice is a great way to build affinity.

You Have Junk-Food Bags in Your Car Too!

It was the moment I was dreading: Katie, the pony-tailed carpool mom, was peering inside my minivan as she buckled her daughter into the car seat for the ride to preschool. We were just getting the carpool thing started, having learned on the first day that our families live near each other. "How cool is that?" Katie said with a grin. "What's cool?" I asked, smiling tentatively. She replied, "I'm so glad you have a couple of fast-food bags in your car. It makes me feel so much better about the state of my own car." Whew, that was a relief! My car will never win any cleanliness awards, and it felt good that Katie wasn't about to pass judgment. In fact, her comment was quite the ice breaker. In one fell swoop, Katie declared she was imperfect, a little messy, kind of easygoing, and well aware of the difficulty of keeping a family minivan in pristine condition. (My van hasn't been pristine since we drove it off the car lot.) From that moment on, the two of us were fast friends. We seemed to be on the same wavelength in many ways, not just in our inability to maintain a clutter-free vehicle. Katie was refreshingly open about her foibles, quirks, and imperfections, which made me feel like I could be myself around her. Be yourself. Be real. And potential friends will feel at ease in your company.

Reestablish Ties with Old Friends

When I speak to moms groups about the importance of keeping up with old pals, those listening inevitably get wistful looks on their faces. One of the questions I always ask is this: "Which one pal of yours do you wish you could reconnect with most of all?" Inevitably, every mom in the room can think of at least one—usually more than one—amigo she hasn't talked to in years, a kindred spirit she misses all the time.

When I asked that question, I know a face came to your mind too. Maybe she was your high school partner in crime, the one who knew you when you had a crush on that hottie in science lab. (You just saw a photo of him at a wedding, and you're dying to dish with someone who knew him back then about his unfortunate case of baldness. And chubbiness. And complete lack of sex appeal.) Or perhaps the face you saw in your mind's eye was that of a college roommate, someone with whom you used to giggle and snort half the night away. There's simply nothing like an old friend.

"Even if our lives take unexpected turns and we are separated by time or geography from those women who shared our childhoods, we never lose the impact they have had in our lives," write Carmen Berry and Tamara Traeder in *Girlfriends: Invisible Bonds, Enduring Ties.* "We take these girlfriends with us each and every day, in our memories as well as in warp and weft of our personalities."[2]

142

Yet it's so easy to let those essential, priceless relationships lie fallow, especially when we become mothers. If you are lonesome for an old pal who knew you when you had braces on your teeth, who dotted your *i*'s with little hearts, and who used to be able to finish your sentences, there's only one course of action: find her ASAP and don't let her go again. Chances are excellent she's been thinking about you too. Call her up and tell her you want to be pals again, even if it's by phone and email for the next five years. Google the girl if you have completely lost track of her, or ask your mom to ask around about her mom, and so on. She can be found! It just may take a little elbow grease on your end.

And when you do reestablish those ties, keep up your end of the friendship! Yes, you're a busy mom with twin three-year-olds whom you are trying to keep from running onto the highway or eating the Christmas poinsettia. True, she's a bond trader whose job you don't even fully understand (you can't even balance your checkbook). But those old connections are strong. And it only takes a couple of minutes per week to zip off an email here and there.

The best tip I can give you for re-cementing a friendship? Make phone dates. My girlfriend Becky and I talk on the phone about three times a year, for about an hour each time. Once every other year or so I'm lucky enough to see her for a day or two at her family's cottage, which happens to be two hours from my parents in Canada. Other than those concentrated times, the Bec and the Lor rely on supershort emails to mark a birthday or a thought wave ("I was thinking about that one time at the lake when you ..."). When I recently ran into Mr.-Baldy-who-dumped-me-fifteen-years-ago, there was no one who could have

143

appreciated the situation like the Bec. We both juggle work and children, and sometimes the last thing we have time for is a lavish phone conversation or even a one-sentence email. But we make time, and that's meant the difference between having her in my life and wondering evermore what became of my beautiful, hilarious, kooky old roomie. Make keeping in touch a high priority. Treat phone dates like sacred appointments, and schedule an hour into your planner once a month or so to catch up with the women who nourish your soul and feed your heart.

Sticky Subjects

Oy vey! There's nothing that can derail a potentially great friendship like that bad apple called mommy competitiveness and the friction that arises when two moms make different parenting choices with their little ones. Listen up as the great and wonderful panel chicks weigh in on secret sensitivities, what they fear could drive a wedge between them and their friends, and how they really feel about those oh-so-sticky subjects.

Jen T.: I think that when you are a new mother you are more sensitive. I hated people saying what their kids were doing in comparison with mine. Now I couldn't care less. I know that motherhood has made me thicker skinned, but I do try to appreciate that other mothers wouldn't want me to compare my child with theirs. If they make the comment on how their child is possibly lacking, I try to boost them up a little and say that no one is going to be the wiser in two years. If they are bragging about the success of their children, I truly am happy for them. I know that the gap between most of our kids will close, so it wouldn't even be accurate to compare the kids right now anyway.

Christy: The whole discipline issue seems tight with some of my mom friends, like how much discipline to apply or when to apply it. A certain other mom just lets her kids get away with things or act in a way that I would *never* let my children act. On the other hand, she is the mom that helped me the most when I had my firstborn. She was great with being able to answer questions about breast-feeding, teething, and so on because she was going through it seven months ahead of me.

Cheryl: I try not to be a know-it-all, but that's so hard when my children and I are perfect and others are so screwed up! I'm joking, of course. Seriously, though, I'm trying to listen more and judge less. My kids aren't perfect—I'm under no delusion that they are. And generally any time I start bragging about them, they'll do something in public to take me down about ten pegs.

Amy: I guess the biggest challenges I've had to handle with other moms are health care issues—whether to immunize or not and antibiotics and such. On the flip side, I have had so much encouragement and advice from my friends on issues like breast-feeding, illness, and discipline problems.

Brenna: TV time when at friends' houses is my sticky topic in regard to my friends and their kids. Ben generally doesn't watch more than an hour of TV per day, and it's a preapproved video or program. At others' houses it's on all the time, and whatever goes . . . yikes!

Kim: Sometimes when I hear where another child is developmentally compared to my child, I feel a bit competitive, and I try to work on whatever it is—ABCs, writing, counting—with my own child. I guess I do have to say I take pride in knowing where my child is developmentally at times. I don't think that I try to rub this in or brag, though.

On the flip side, although tension can arise over differing parental philosophies, mommy pals can provide phenomenal support for those days you want to run down the street screaming (and possibly naked) when your preschooler is jumping on your last nerve. The panel concurs. Whether our friends are helping make us better moms or just making our day, we couldn't live without them!

Cheryl: It's nice to have mom friends who've been there, done that, and survived to tell the tale. I've gotten great ideas and encouragement from my friends—as well as occasional babysitting offers! They've all been a huge blessing to me.

Jodi: I have friends with children a couple of years older than my kids, and they help me keep the phases and seasons of particular annoying behaviors in perspective—for instance, the whole issue of potty training. I have twins, and I just do not feel like potty training, so I am going to wait until they cannot stand soiled diapers anymore and have them take a big part in the potty-training process. Why make more work for myself than I really need to?

Ann: Most of my friends who are moms have children slightly older than my kids. They are instrumental in what I call the "mommy reality check." For everything from being warned about a young boy's fascination with running around the house wearing underwear and winter boots (during the height of summer, of course), to gentle reassurances that this too will pass, my friends help me stay sane.

Brenna: My friends help me realize I need to let go of some stuff and let the kids make a mess—it's fun! They also provide so much support. It's great being able to talk about my frustrations and fears.

Mary Jo: My friends are an invaluable source of information on ways to deal with new issues that pop up each day. With a preschooler I haven't run into too much of the competitive thing—at least not on my part. That may arise as Josephine and Louisa continue to grow, I can imagine.

Friendships Gone Wrong

Keep your friends at all costs? Well, maybe keep them at *most* costs. If a friend is too braggy about her tykes or she's not keeping up her end of the relationship, your connection is weakened but probably not beyond repair. What can really rupture a friendship is this kind of one-sidedness for years on end, although early intervention can put the

Hello, Dolly

What does your sweetie want to be when she grows up? Anything—the world is her oyster! One way she can figure out how grown-ups act and behave is by playing with her dolls. A baby doll, then, becomes her baby, whom she cradles, feeds, changes, and generally nurtures the stuffing out of. Your little guy may or may not be into the doll scene, but if he is, he's simply hooking into a huge developmental theme. Nothing facilitates imaginary scenarios like dolls, stuffed animals, and action figures.

Around the age of four or so, your daughter may eschew her precious teddy or baby doll in favor of more sophisticated, poseable dolls like Polly Pockets. This way she can act out various tableaus she's seen unfold in real life, using her dolls as the actors in her mind's teleplay.

If you walk by your daughter's room and hear her give her doll a "time-out" for "sassing," the scene may be all too familiar. Or let's say your son is "saving" you from the bad monsters, waving his Spider-Man action figure around. (He's never seen the movie, of course; he just loves the

wheels back on before you two skid off track completely. Get up the guts to tell her, in a nonthreatening way, how she's hurt you, and hope and pray she'll receive your message and change her ways.

action figure!) Wonder why your kids enact these elaborate vignettes? Pure instinct, says child development expert John W. Lee. "In addition to the fun and enjoyment this brings to young children, doll play also serves beneficial developmental purposes by allowing kids to work out their emotions in a safe context. Scolding their baby doll or stuffed animal lets children work out their feelings without involving another child," he says.[3]

Like the early clay dolls found in Greek, Roman, and Egyptian cultures, your little one's dolls spark an amazing world of make-believe.

Look for dolls that come from your child's same peer group. Instead of buying a bling-bling fashion Barbie, choosing a child doll is far more beneficial. Says Lee, "This really opens the door for them to work out situations that they are in currently as well as in situations that they may find themselves in the near future."[4]

Besides, we want to keep those little girls little as long as possible!

But . . . when a so-called pal is harshly critical of you or, worse, your family members, or she is so needy all the time that you feel positively sucked dry after getting together, it might be time to consider "breaking up."

We may be one-half of an off-kilter friendship for a time, so we might do some good for the other person, but that doesn't mean we should endure all kinds of pain and drain over the long haul. "As mothers, the demands on our time and our emotions are already so great that we have to be especially diligent not to entertain any friendships that drain our energies, drag us down, or burden us unnecessarily," says Mary Byers.[5]

I've been entangled in friendships that seemed more like counseling services than give-and-take relationships. I've had a couple of women friends who seemed to want far more from me than I could possibly give—100 percent takers. And once, a friend was so possessive and exclusive that I felt like a person gasping for oxygen. Of those three women, one is still in my life, and the relationship has improved dramatically with hard-won boundaries in place.

Mary Byers is right. With all we moms have on our plates, emotionally at the very least, we can't afford to have skewed relationships. Don't let go of friendships easily, as they can and should be positive, life-giving endeavors. But do release relationships that are toxic, and you will find more energy for refreshing, healthful ones. Like Angela Thomas Gruffy says about a poisonous pal, "I would not give her permission to walk around in my soul."[6] Watch who's walking around in your soul, and be smart about who you invite in!

FUN THINGS

Cheryl really needed her friends after the Crazy Daisy Sprinkler incident!

It was a hot day in July . . . how's that for a start? It was lunchtime, and my then four-year-old son, Nathanael, wanted to play in the sprinkler and kiddie pool before his nap. I just wanted to finish my lunch in peace while Adrielle napped. So out he went into the fenced backyard with me checking on him every eight to ten minutes or so. The first eight minutes go by, so I look out—he's washing his Cozy Coupé. Fine. The second eight minutes elapse—he's watering the herbs by the garage. The third eight minutes—still watering herbs. Things were a little soggy but OK. The fourth eight minutes—he's in the pool. OK. But wait. Why is the water on in the garage? When I asked Nathanael, his reply was a blank look, so I went in the garage to discover the Crazy Daisy Sprinkler flower head propped in the only open window of the Honda Accord. Every surface of the car was soaked—roof, walls, dashboard, pockets for cassettes on the doors, car seats, rear window speakers—with water dripping into the trunk. There was one and a half inches of water on the floor in the backseat. He was sent up to bed for an extended nap time while I spent the next hour and a half having to wet-vac the car.

The car didn't really dry out for two weeks—and that was with the doors and windows open while baking in the hot summer sun! Part of me wanted to kill him, and part of me thought, *Well, this will just be the funny story you tell about him until the day he gets married.* That was three years ago, and trust me, he's already added a few more stories to the repertoire!

(For more on Nathanael's "deluxe" preschool years, turn to pages 174–75.)

12

MOM AND DAD GOT IT GOIN' ON

Revamping your love life

AH, YOUR MAN. What a man! He's not Orlando Bloom in the abs department (or—let's be honest—any department), and he doesn't have Hugh Grant's stammering charm or yummy accent. But he does listen to you unload about the tedious details of your relationship with your sister. He's your always-available companion on Friday nights when the sitter is busy and Blockbuster is out of every movie except *Joe Dirt*. He vanquishes spiders, cracks open the spaghetti-sauce jar, and doesn't gripe too much about moving the furniture around in the living room. He's the only other person who really understands how cute the kids are (even when they're being beastly).

So he's a terrific guy, a "catch" (so your single girlfriend has said more than once as she enviously regards your apparent domestic bliss). But girlfriend, if your husband is such a dishy, dreamy dude, why are you not entering into nakedness with him on a regular basis? Hmmm?

Actually, if you don't know, I may have a few notions why. When I wrote my last book, *We Should Do This More Often: A Parents' Guide to Romance, Passion, and Other Pre-Child Activities You Vaguely Recall*, I researched the whole realm of moms and sexuality extensively. I mean, I *researched*, if you catch my drift. (I also looked at a bunch of books, magazines, and Internet articles.)

What I found was incontrovertible evidence that (a) there's a whole bunch of reasons young mothers lose their mojo, and (b) there's a whole bunch of reasons they need to get their mojo back. What's mojo, you ask? It's spice, passion, an abiding interest in nookie that doesn't die down completely, even when your kids take turns having the stomach flu. What do the kiddies have to do with your mojo? Everything. Those little *hijos* and *hijas* are determined to throw a big wet blankie all over your mojo. The munchkins want you to never leave the house with your guy; instead, they prefer you to stay home and cater to their every whim.

What they don't know is that they will feel more secure, content, and otherwise happy if you are cultivating your passionate life with your husband. You two are the bricks and mortar of your family, and when you neglect the romance, passion, and razzle-dazzle in your union, things can become pretty shaky.

So why don't you shake things up in a good way? I've said this before, and I'll say it again: your red-hot mama is in there somewhere. Let's get busy and find her!

154

But, But, But . . .

"See, Lorilee, I'm willing to find my red-hot mama (presumably she knows where my mojo is too). But you know, our parents don't live in town so we don't go out much, I've gained all this baby fat and feel as unsexy as can be, and besides, I'm tuckered out at the end of the day!"

Uh-huh, I do see. Sounds like some of the responses I got from my panel when I queried them about this topic: "How do you keep things hot between you and your husband?"

Three women said, "We still don't have it figured out." Christy said, "It's really hard! Especially since I'm breast-feeding again. Night sex usually doesn't work because I'm *sooo* exhausted, and I'm nervous that the baby will wake up by the time we are done and I will not have gotten any sleep!" Carol said, "I would make more time and energy for sex, but my four-year-old is always climbing in bed with us!"

Yes, it's puzzling, it's hard, and it's frustrating, but ladies, it's got to be done. We have got to push through the barriers to a sizzling sex life and make it happen. When we do that, and we reclaim our luscious selves (buried under a baggy sweatshirt, a spit-up rag, and granny panties), the rewards are fantastic.

Take a peek at a few of the emails I've gotten from readers: "I see now that the kids will be fine without me for a few hours. We had so much fun on our date the other night." . . . "We never went anywhere without the kids. But since I booked a room at a B and B [for just the two of us], I feel like a new woman." . . . "My friends teased me when I got your book out of the library. Wait'll I tell them it may have saved my marriage."

I share these testimonial snippets to underscore the wonderful rewards that can be yours if you make a few key changes in your marriage and family life. Cheryl did, and check out the results:

> It took me a good many years to figure this out, pathetically enough, but my husband and I are so much more relaxed and much less crabby after making love. It's not always about "hot" or "sexy" but sheer mental and physical survival. We're more bonded, we're better parents, and we tolerate everything and everyone better. That's much sexier than being stressed-out and crabby, and that can lead to . . ."

You don't have to draw us a picture, Cheryl, but it sounds like things are warm around the old campfire at your house! As Martha would say, "It's a good thing."

How do you get in on this good thing, this reclaiming of sparks, heat, and va-va voom?

Get Those Home Fires Burning

Remember Who the King and Queen Are

Something strange and twisted happens when we have our first baby. Suddenly our priorities flip upside down, and the guy who used to make the earth move under our feet? He can go jump in a lake, for all intents and purposes. Babies need so much from us, very true. But once we get the hang of diapers, feedings, and endless care, we have to tunnel our way back to the man we love. (Your baby's four and you still catch yourself asking your husband if he has to go potty? And is that maternity underwear you're wearing?) It's time to switch gears for your sake, his sake, and your kids' sake. Always keep in mind that your relationship with your husband is the primary one of your family. Essentially, your connection with him is more vital than the bond you have with your kids. Hard to remember, isn't it?

Leave the Castle with the King on a Regular Basis

The royal underlings will kick up a fuss, sure, but they have to learn that Ma and Pa need some time alone to nourish their relationship. Doyle and I have two talkative, active boys who barely let us get a word in edgewise most of the time. Uninterrupted time for chats? Not happening. Leisurely, relaxed interludes? Not on planet Craker. So we phone our trusty fifteen-year-old babysitter, Helen, and she comes over and fixes Mac-n-Cheese, plays Sorry, and watches *The Incredibles* while Doyle and I venture out. Dinner, the movies, the park, the beach, Cold Stone Creamery—really, wherever the kids aren't is instantly a romantic location. We unwind, laugh, flirt, and, by golly, we finish our sentences. And then twice a year or so, we leave for a longer, more restorative, glorious weekend away.

Like Jen T., you must try it yourself:

I have no problem leaving my kids for a weekend. Couples need to remember why they married one another in the first place. If you are getting annoyed with every little thing that your husband is doing, I suggest getting away together ... *without the kids!* We are fortunate that we can schedule time away every three months or so to Toronto for our business. This allows us to tear it up a little together and feel young again.

The benefits of time away together are manifold. Yes, you'll feel young again, revitalized, and much more in sync with your "luvah." If you still don't believe me, take the time to read through Sharon's fascinating story of how a four-day getaway transformed her marriage. (Hint: it's not what you expect.)

I asked Bruce your question about keeping things hot in our relationship. His response was, "Go to Tennessee!" We just recently had gone to the Smokey Mountains for our ten-year anniversary. We *sooo* had looked forward to some "alone time" with no interruptions and to being able to give the best part of our day to each other. (We both tend to go comatose shortly after the kids go to bed, so "our time" is not always the best for "alone time.") So Bruce and I rented the most romantic cabin you could imagine and proceeded to have one of the most volatile, passionate fights of our marriage—on day two! I was very hurt, angry, and sad that we were wasting this long-awaited trip by fighting. I don't think that I had been that mad in my whole life. We verbalized and verbalized again our feelings, sometimes thinking we were not getting anywhere.

To make a long story short, by day four God brought us to the end of ourselves and truly gave us a miracle. We were brought to a new understanding of the issue we were fighting about. The result? Reconciliation, warmth, and wonderful, passionate "alone time"! I mean better than ever. Really. And not just for one day!

Now we look at the fight as such a gift from God. If we had begun that fight at home, we would still be feuding.

You know, at home there can be a lack of eye contact, no snuggling, some attempts at trying to talk it out in hushed tones while expecting the children to climb up the stairs at any minute and witness World War III in their living room. If we had had this argument at home, it would have been a long, cold war. I think God brought us to the Smokies to jump over a hurdle in our marriage that could have taken years to "figure out" if we were to do it during the normal day-to-day living.

Anyway, the moral of this story for us is twofold: God knows what he is doing and will bless us beyond what we think, and . . . *get away together*. I believe it gives God a chance to work in our marriages (and sex lives) in a way that is truly impossible when we are in the rigors of the daily Mom and Dad responsibilities. Even though the majority of our last trip was spent yelling at each other, I wouldn't trade it now for anything.

At Least Wear a Lacy Somethin' Underneath

Yes, you've gained weight, and your breasts ain't what they used to be before they were employed as milking machines. Body image is a huge deterrent to a great sex life (read more about it in chap. 13), and we have to be intentional and aggressive about accepting our physiques. I did say "we." Through the process I describe in the body image section, I come to terms with my size twelve, not overly toned physique. So I work on making it better, and in the meantime, I prefer my boudoir lighting on the dimmer side!

And then there's what we put on our bodies. If you dress like a nun, under the mistaken impression moms aren't allowed to be cute or feminine, you'll feel about as sexy as Sister Agnes. Even wearing a pair of naughty undies from time to

159

time, say, under your preschool picnic attire, will attune you to the fact that you are a sexual person, even though your son just wiped his ketchup-covered hands on your sweater. Yanking out an older, flimsy article of seduction is not a bad idea either, and it makes a nice change of pace from that Winnie the Pooh nightshirt you've been sporting. Just ask Kim: "We've both been so busy lately, but when the spirit does move I put on a sexy nightie for him with some lacy undies, and that pretty much does the trick." Work at body acceptance, perk up your wardrobe—outerwear and under-wear—and see if your love life doesn't perk up too.

If You Wait for the Mood to Strike . . .

You'll be waiting until the cows come home. Just do it. Even if your mood is not quite the raging desire you were hoping for, if you get a little twinkling that a romp could be fun, bash ahead and hope for the best! I'm serious now. New research strongly suggests that we were wrong all these years: we don't have to wait until we feel some kind of big urge to merge. Once we get going, the urge will follow.

"How many people who jog feel like doing it before they start?" asks Michele Weiner Davis, super-duper marriage therapist and author of *The Sex-Starved Marriage*. "But once they get started, they feel pretty good."[1]

It's not rocket science, my friends, but revving up the lusty engines takes some effort, reprioritizing, and a wee slip of lace here and there. You can do it! Alicia did. "Spontaneity is the key for us in keeping things hot," she says. "We are remembering to put each other first and remembering most of all to have some fun!"

If Your Curious Offspring Bust In

Three seems to be the age when kids begin to point and prod and verbalize their thoughts about their parents' fascinating bodies. Boy, do they ever. (Ask me sometime about the most mortifying blurt in Craker history, when one of my kids semi-yelled, in a restaurant, a question about the female anatomy.) Of course, it's normal for family members to see each other in various states of undress at times, and your child won't be permanently scarred if he sees you in the nude. But even if you're uncomfortable going au naturel, don't show it—he might start to associate nakedness with shame. Explain that the human body is natural, beautiful, and nothing to be ashamed of, but Mommy likes to keep her private parts, well, private.[2]

FUN THINGS

"I don't think we will ever forget when our son was three," says one flabbergasted mom. "We didn't shut the door, and we were so *involved* we didn't hear him come in. Next thing you know, my husband gets hit on the butt with a baseball bat! Really ruined the moment, to say the least!" (from *We Should Do This More Often*)

13

LIKE THE SKIN YOU'RE IN

Improving your post-baby body image

ONE OF KATHI's chief memories of growing up was watching her mom get up from the dinner table, night after night, and hit the floor for a brisk round of stomach crunches. As you can imagine, Kathi's own body image was shaped by the indelible picture of her average-sized mom punishing herself for eating a regular meal. I am wincing as I write these words, but unfortunately, this scenario is not uncommon. Our culture's obsession with thin bodies began about the time our moms were raising us.

Alison remembers her mom, circa 1975 or so, plagued by a distorted view of her own body. "My mom, who seemed just right to me, was always talking about how fat she was," says Alison. "I remember saying, 'You're not fat, Mom, but Dad is.' (He had a paunch.) There is a Polaroid picture from that time. My mother is in the center, smiling, so beautiful. She is slender and radiant, unbelievably the mother of four little ones. The caption at the bottom, in her writing, reads, 'Only five more pounds to go!'"

This distortion filtered down to little Alison, who always had, she says, "a quiet uneasiness that I would be fat too."

Did you know that pregnancy and its effects on our figure induce more "disordered eating" than at any other time of life? That means we as young *madres* are more prone to a disturbed view of food and a hatred for our changing shapes than even teenagers, who are famous for eating disorders! Why? Well, for one, we usually pack on a few pounds when we become preggers, and getting our bodies back afterward is sometimes not even a possibility.

According to Debra Waterhouse, author of *Outsmarting the Female Fat Cell—After Pregnancy*, our fat cells enlarge like crazy after giving birth and then fight us to the death before burning away. Our metabolism slows by 15 to 25 percent postpartum, and baby-related stress (remember colic?) can lead to binges. Plus, with the advent of the munchkins, we don't have time to exercise as much as we used to—or at all! On the other hand, an Australian study showed that moms who dieted had greater body dissatisfaction than moms who didn't![1]

To recap: moms are less than psyched about their weight gain, of course, and now have all these factors conspiring against ever becoming fit and trim again (or maybe for the first time). No wonder 96 percent of women have some sort of complaint in regard to their bods! Yikes! Let's change that, starting now. Let's transform our thinking, our hearts, and our bodies. We will benefit so much, and our kids—especially our girls—will too.

Ten Tips for a Better Mommy Body Image

1. Quit Thinking You Need to Be a Size Two

Recently I interviewed the comic Kathi Griffin for an entertainment piece for *The Grand Rapids Press*. The in-your-face redhead was blunt as usual about every topic under the sun, especially the difficulty of fitting her thin-but-not-thin-enough frame into Hollywood's absurd standard shape. "I'm a size six, and in Hollywood I'm a big fat cow!" she said, disgusted. (I've got you doubled, sister, but I digress.) "But I have a theory why everyone is a size zero or a size two: they're hungry! Hungry!"

I laughed at her obviously humorous statement, but later her words sunk in, and it occurred to me that she was dead serious. The glitzy waifs of Tinseltown apparently conduct their lives with a perpetually growling tummy, spinning heads, and zero pleasure from food, one of God's great gifts. Who knows where these women get their energy to work eighteen-hour days on movie sets, not to mention for the grueling Pilates routines that give them such sleek abs? It's a mystery, but the point is that *these* are our role models for what an ideal shape looks like. These beautiful, glamorous, bony, and hungry ragamuffins are, somehow, perceived in our culture as being perfect.

I don't know about you, but walking around hungry all day, every day, is not my idea of a good time. God wired us to want and enjoy food! Now, we've gone a bit hog wild in this supersized day and age, and inhaling a bag of brownies isn't any better than nibbling at sprouts. Our first step needs to be consciously filtering the messages from our culture. Aggressively say no to unnaturally thin ideals, and shoot instead for health and energy, even if that process doesn't lead you to slip on a size two Dolce & Gabbana frock the next time you're at the Oscars—or at the preschool picnic. Ask for God's wisdom as you set out to sift through these cultural news flashes that tell you you're not good enough if you're not thin enough.

2. Just Say No to Slabs of Food

I love food, and for me, measuring and weighing ounces of meat or cubes of cheese is enough to make me nuts. I tried a big-name diet program last year that convinced me once and for all that dieting was not for me. The program was three weeks of carb-free, fun-free, pleasure-free living that finally resulted in a meager weight loss that doesn't bear mentioning. The "counselors" at this diet program would always scratch their heads in bewilderment as to why I wasn't losing weight. "Are you sure you didn't have more than the allotted carbs on Tuesday?" the lady said, leafing through my diet diary with a fine-toothed comb. "Oh, look here! Here it is! You ate *four* low-fat Triscuits. You are only allowed *three*. See? And on Wednesday night you had tomato sauce, which is full of salt. Sometimes it takes a few days for that sodium to leave your system. See?" All I could see was that, for all my misery, I felt hungry all the time, I couldn't partake of meals when we were dining at friends' houses, and truthfully, I would have happily throttled my diet adviser right then and there. (This lady, a "deluxe" pear-shaped grandma,

166

had told me upon arriving—by way of encouragement, no doubt—that she had weighed the same as me before joining the program. Wasn't that just great?)

Nope, not for me, this business of being scolded for one extra cracker and being made to feel like a freak of nature because I couldn't lose weight. Remember the Australian study? My body dissatisfaction was at an all-time high at the conclusion of those doleful three weeks. What I decided then and there was that the only way to manage my eating was with some portion control, making the effort to keep my piece of lasagna the size of a portion, not a slab. At the drive-through, instead of a Big Mac and large fries, I started getting a cheeseburger and a diet Coke. Sometimes I would also get the small fries, or else a Happy Meal, which is basically the same thing—with a toy. (I save the toys from "my" Happy Meal for a treat at some point when one of my kids deserves one.)

In her book *French Women Don't Get Fat*, author Mireille Guiliano says the ladies of France would sooner climb the Eiffel Tower in stiletto heels than go on a low-carb diet. Why? They would never dream of depriving themselves that way, yet they don't, as a rule, pack it on like we North Americans do. The upshot? Learn to enjoy your food without overdoing it, and make portion savvy a part of your lifestyle.

3. Rev Up Your Metabolism (without Hitting the Gym)

One easy way to do something good for your body (which will encourage good feelings) is to tweak your metabolism and fat-burning mechanisms. Experts say three servings of calcium per day, in the form of low-fat milk, yogurt, or cheese, will kick-start your fat-burning process. Easy enough, eh? It took me about two weeks to get in the groove of three-a-day milk products, but once I did, it became second nature. Now I'm not only speeding up the old fat elimination—cool thing that is—but I'm also benefiting my bones, for now and especially for the future. To kick it up a notch, buy a set of free weights and download a home workout plan you can do right away. Three times a week or so, I do my free weight routine as I'm watching TV with Doyle at the end of the day. Those in the know contend the more we build those muscles, the more fat we burn—even while we sleep! And again, weight training protects your bones, so one day you'll be kicking some granny booty at shuffleboard. Implementing these two simple changes into your lifestyle will bring all kinds of health and wellness bennies your way. Green tea also kicks up your fat-burning machines and is loaded with antioxidants.

4. Don't Get Your Shorts in a Knot

True, the cat's climbing the drapes, your five-year-old just announced his tummy feels sick, and half an hour ago you and your man traded snide remarks about an upcoming mother-in-law visit. But it's not going to do you or your body any good if you get your shorts in a knot, physiologically speaking. Pay attention to your stress levels. When you notice that you've got some tension going on, take the time to breathe deeply a few times. That will help in the short run, but for the long haul, it's great for your sense of well-being to carve out time for Mom. Go out for coffee with a giggly friend. Immerse your weary bones in a bubble bath.

168

Listen to music that perks up your mood. All of these self-nurturing strategies will go a long way toward reducing your stress level. (More on self-care in the Mommy Spa section on pages 177–82.)

5. Work It, Sister

Don't throw tomatoes at me, girls, but some form of exercise is in order for basic health. And don't you think exercising is way more fun than dieting? Now, if you're shaking your head vehemently and breaking out in a cold sweat, it's because you've come to associate exercise with torture. Don't base your whole view of this realm on that one time your best friend dragged you to a spinning class (a high-intensity stationary bike-riding class) and you almost passed out from sheer exhaustion and pain. Try to think of exercise as *moving*. Motion. Action. Anything that gets you up and propelling yourself around is good—for a start. It doesn't have to be awful either. Walking extra briskly as you take your kids to the park qualifies. Playing Frisbee in the park with your husband also fits the bill. Swimming is great for your body, and you don't even sweat (that you know of).

The basic reason to exercise is for your health. It adds years to your life span, not to mention giving you an extra boost of energy, stamina, and stress busting for day-to-day living. I had a gym membership for four and a half years, up until about nine months ago. I loved that gym! I could hit the elliptical machine for forty-five minutes while drinking my water and catching a morning talk show I could never watch at home because it interfered with my son's favorite show. But I quit going to the gym because it was a luxury, and luxuries didn't mesh well with the foreign adoption we were in the middle of financing. So now I have to get creative. Running up and down the stairs five to ten times is one way I get my heart rate up. Jumping rope for a couple of minutes at a time also works, although the rope sometimes scrapes the ceiling annoyingly. I recently bought a mini stair-stepper, which is small, is portable, and allows me to sneak in a little exercise while I'm watching *American Idol* or something. All that to say, if I can work out in a smallish house with three small kids in the middle of winter, you can do it too!

6. "Housewife Wins In-Home Stanley Cup"

This, girls, is mommy multitasking at its finest. Deborah Norville, journalistic superstar and anchor of *Inside Edition*, was being interviewed about balancing life, work, and kids. This smart cookie said the most amazing thing. Instead of coming home after a long day's work and hitting the treadmill—like so many svelte ladies in the public eye—Norville said she chased her tykes around the house. "That way I could be a fun mom and sneak in a little exercise too," she said. What a fab-oo idea! Moms as a rule don't have gym memberships or time to do a daily workout video. But we do have time to play a fast-paced game of "Mommy is a crazy gorilla who wants to eat you for dessert, so you'd better run." Try sprinting a few laps up and down the stairs in hot pursuit of a certain four-year-old who looks yummy to Gorilla Woman. You'll huff and puff, believe me. And the big bonus here is that your preschooler will think you are awesome.

My friend Kathy G. is the matriarch of a hockey-crazed clan in Minnesota. Instead of feeling cooped up in the twenty-below-zero weather the other day, Kathy got her heart rate up as she played with her boys. "Yesterday we set up a huge, metal roller hockey net in our living room and skated on paper plates," she said. "Caleb loved being goalie, while Tyler and I faked each other out on the 'ice.' By the way, the large, thick paper platters—perfect for my size nines—provide quite the workout as they don't have the smooth bottoms. You should try it. Buh-bye, thigh-master; hello, Chinet!"

7. Tell Your Thighs You Love Them

Your body is prey to hideous critiques from someone who should know better: you! We deflate whatever positive body image we may have with our constant slams to ourselves about our mommy shapes. "Yuck!" "Oh, my thighs are gross!" "Could I possibly *have* more cellulite?" "I can't believe how flat I am—I look like a twelve-year-old boy!" Add them up, ten times a day, seven days a week, and you have a monumental amount of insults being hurled at you—from you! So you have to toughen up, bite your tongue, and not indulge in negative self-talk. Over the long haul, it's positively toxic, and it ultimately undermines all your best efforts to improve your body and body image. Think about it: you would never allow your child or even a friend to talk about her body that way, so why do you tear yourself down so much?

Send good messages instead. I'm not talking about sheer denial of the facts: "My, my, don't we look like we jumped out of the Victoria's Secret catalog today?" Rather, accentuate the positive, and focus on that: "I do have cute knees." "My waist is looking trimmer." "My arms are starting to look more toned since I've been working with free weights." Trust me, this is one component of the better-body-image plan that must be in place. Shut down any insults you are lobbing at your body, and practice replacing them with kinder, gentler messages.

8. Don't Drag Your Husband into It

"Do you think this dress makes me look too fat?" When you ask your guy that question, all he can do is inwardly groan and tell you what he thinks you want to hear. An old boss of mine would get this question thrown at him from his wife all the time, and he concluded there was just no good answer. "What do I tell her?" he asked, exasperated. "That the dress or pants or whatever make her look 'just fat enough'?" Girls, we need to resist that powerful urge to drag our husbands into our body-image "stuff." When the question "Does this make me look fat?" is on the tip of your tongue, stop it in its tracks! Guys abhor anything to do with that line of questioning. They would rather be subjected to watching reality dating shows than be dragged into discussions about the size of your butt. I have a theory that when we do air our insecurities like that, our men start to think that, yes, we do look a little chub-city lately. A far more upbeat approach would be to smile with confidence and say, "How do I look?" They are men, after all, not girlfriends. We usually do have to fish just a teeny bit for feedback! Or, since men are usually not as intuitive as we would like them to be, our husbands occasionally require us to tell them flat-out what we need. "Hon, I've been feeling not so positive about my body since the baby came. I could really use some positive comments here and there."

9. Dress as if You Like Your Body

This is probably another whole book, but so often, when women become moms, they begin to dress like, well, *their* moms. It's the oddest thing. Pre-baby, a young woman can be altogether hip and happening, but post-baby? She's suddenly wearing frumpy cardigans with cutesy apples, pumpkins, or kittens appliquéd into the knit. Real cute if you're seven—or seventy. Yes, the bod isn't what it used to be, but does that mean you have to dress like you're middle-aged? Baggy, huge sweatshirts and dowdy turtlenecks with seasonal embroidery do nothing for you. And don't get me started on the granny panties! I'm not suggesting you wear plunging necklines and miniskirts as you're grocery shopping; modesty is always a good idea. The thing is, when you dress poky you feel poky, which just adds to a negative body image. Check out magazine articles about dressing well for your body type. There's got to be at least one or two such articles out on newsstands in any given month, so great is the demand for help in that area. Miss Pear Shape here just got some nifty ideas in *Redbook* for a new spring outfit that won't embellish the *bellish*, if you know what I mean.

Weed out the matronly articles of clothing, and replace them with things that fit and make you feel perkier. Save the granny panties for when you're actually a granny—or maybe not. When I gave my body-image talk to a MOPS group recently, a seventy-four-year-old mentor mom stood up, yanked up the top of her undies, and revealed a snazzy little purple lace number. Well, she brought down the house, and she underscored the message that you don't have to look like a matron, even if you are one!

173

10. Reshape from the Inside Out

You can pump iron, drink gallons of low-fat milk, eat salads until you turn green, and wear a thong every day, but if you don't address the spiritual matter at the core of a poor body image, you're always going to be dissatisfied and insecure. Ask God to forgive you for disliking the body he made with so much love and care. Pray that he will show you the root emotional cravings that cause you to turn to food. Invite the one who knit you together in your mother's womb (see Ps. 139:13) to reshape your body image from the inside out. Be honest with him, because he already knows how you feel about that double chin. "Be transformed by the renewing of your mind," the Bible says in Romans 12:2. You can't refresh your thinking without your Father's transforming power. Only he can change you so that one day, when you read that your body is "fearfully and wonderfully made" (Ps. 139:14), you'll really believe that it's true.

FUN THINGS

More from Cheryl's journal about her wild and woolly preschooler, Nathanael!

I keep a journal for each of my kids of the "cute" things they do and say. "Memorable" would probably be a better adjective. I was looking at Nathanael's journal today, and I have about ten pages of stories from June to November 2001 (age three and nine months to four and three months). He was *so* creatively naughty. Never malicious. Very creative. Boundary tester. For him, not forbidden meant fair game.

Here's a sampling from that nutty summer when N was four:

June 26: Crazy Daisy Sprinkler episode

July 5: N pees in the heating duct next to the toilet (because he "wanted to be naughty").

Also July 5, later that day: I find a pen and the fact that he had written all over his mattress pad. Before I lambaste him he points to an X in his drawings and says, "That's the cross Jesus died on." So much for getting mad!

July 9: N finds scissors and brings them to his room while I put Adrielle to bed. He "fringes" the mattress pad and cuts a blankie, a library book, a ribbon on a photo album, the wallpaper border, etc.

Late July: N goes to visit grandparents for a week to give us a break. Very first morning, 7:00 a.m., Grandma and Grandpa lying in bed with bedroom door open so they can hear when Nathanael stirs in room across hall. Doorbell rings for back door. Stealth boy was already awake and outside. Put them on their toes for the week!

August 13: My father's sixtieth birthday. He calls unexpectedly at 5:30 p.m. to see if he can come for dinner and spend the night—he'll be there in a half hour. I'm scurrying to pull together a dinner and pick up house. I put eight-month-old Adrielle in stroller outside (brakes on) with Nathanael, give him some bubbles, and tell him to blow bubbles for her for a few minutes. Look outside a few minutes later; he's running around and she looks "sweaty." He had dumped the whole bottle of bubbles on her head, so I add "give baby bath" to my to-do list.

August 14: I decide he's definitely going to preschool that fall—three times a week!

14

MOMMY MINISPAS

Taking a load off

OK, so a guy named Sven is not giving you a blissful, re-laxing Swedish massage, murmuring to you now and again in a great Swedish accent. (The closest you've gotten to Swedish anything are those meatball leftovers from last night's dinner.) But you can still carve out little pockets of time in your hectic mommy life. In fact, you need to create times to indulge in simple pleasures, relaxing endeavors, and replenishing pursuits. You don't even have to leave the building. Your revitalization plan could mean getting ready for bed at 7:00 p.m., with a fan on for white noise and a can't-put-it-down novel, or listening to that same book on tape as you lounge around, cucumber slices in your eye sockets. Your re-creation begins when you permit yourself to have some "me time." Think you don't deserve to take care of yourself on a regular basis? Check out "Heck Yeah, I Want a Medal" on pages 38 and 60, and get back to me after I'm done waxing my eyebrows.

Ten Ways to Restore and Revive

1. Do Nothing

"I try to practice the art of simply existing for at least five minutes a day," says Mary Byers, author of *The Mother Load.* "It's difficult. But spending time doing nothing often produces great results: ideas flow, thanksgiving wells up in my soul. Peace settles in, energy is restored. And more than anything, I reconnect with a sense of deep purpose that encouraged me in the first place."[1] When the kids are napping, down for the night, or otherwise occupied, turn off the radio and TV, shut your magazine, and let your mind go long.

2. Read a Book—with No Pictures

How long has it been since you got lost in the pages of a juicy novel or a fascinating biography of someone you admire? Hit the sack twenty to thirty minutes earlier to make daily progress on your reading. You'll find you can't wait for that time each day to find out what your favorite characters are up to.

3. Read a Glossy Magazine—with Lots of Pictures

My friend Emily likes to hit the local book and coffee mecca with her husband, George, and two tiny tots. She and George take turns riding herd on the kids, and when it's Em's time off? She loses herself in the magazine section for half an hour, leafing through the glossiest, most aesthetically gorgeous mags she can find (and sometimes this means looking at pics of the beautiful people, just to see what they were wearing at the SAG Awards). Throw in a mug of decadently flavored steaming java, and life is deliciously shallow for thirty glorious minutes.

4. Grab a Buddy and See a Chick Flick

Now, I am a movie buff who enjoys serious, award-worthy movies, but sometimes a girl just has to look at some pretty Brits in period costumes declaring their undying love in a colloquial fashion. We women need to bust loose sometimes and giggle helplessly at the capers of a movie couple who must hurdle many silly barriers to get it through their thick skulls that they have the hots for each other. Does your husband balk at too much Julia, Gwyneth, or Reese? Call a friend, get a flick on the calendar, and have big fun for a night!

5. Take In Some Culture

When was the last time you just gazed at a masterpiece in an art museum? I'll bet the last time you were at a museum, it was the children's variety, and you had at least two monkeys hanging on you, pulling you toward different kid-friendly exhibits. Get tickets for a local play or musical. Absorb art for art's sake, and see what grows in your soul.

6. Power Nap

Don't have time for an hour and a half of luscious snoozing? No, of course you don't! But you probably have twenty minutes, which experts say is the optimum amount of time for a midday siesta anyway. (If you've ever lain down for a nap, slept for an hour, and felt worse than you did before lying down, it's because you slept too long.) Get this: by sleeping for twenty minutes, you tap into the power of light sleep. A twenty-minute nap allows you to awaken refreshed because you don't reach stage-three sleep, which is deep sleep. Try power napping—it changed my life!

7. Splurge

I don't know about you, but a little splurge can make me feel positively fizzy. (A big splurge, on the other hand, can make me feel positively dizzy!) Tiny extravagances include yummy-smelling lip balm, hand cream, or small tubes of luxury hair products.

8. Purge

Make like a clutter-buster and start tossing. Pile give-away stuff into big rubber containers and admire your now-available closet space. Throw away twenty pieces of paper, and recycle ten magazines. Pitching stuff out will stream-line your home and your mind. Purging every day will prevent accumulation and the overwhelming feeling that comes with it.

9. Beautify

Once a month or so, do something that makes you feel a little more like a woman. Go for a manicure or set up a home nail salon. Do an in-depth hair conditioning treatment, or whip up one of those home spa treatments and give yourself a facial. Yes, during the day you are a human Kleenex receptacle and Band-Aid dispenser, but at least one night a month you can unleash your inner girlie girl. My thing is coloring my hair. (There, I said it. I am not really a natural "mochachino.") It's not usually a very dramatic change, but I do end up feeling brighter and perkier after an hour in the bathroom, listening to Norah Jones or Diana Krall or Jim Brickman (I'm a sap, what can I say?) and turning my tresses a glamorous shade of java-brown.

Do Try This at Home!

One night when your main man whisks the tykes off for an hour of T-ball or fast food or something, take time to do some home spa action. Light some yummy-scented candles all over your bathroom, and pop in some tunes that make you feel calm and mellow. While the bath water is running, add some luscious bath bubbles or milk in a scent that doesn't compete with the candles. Mix up some oatmeal and olive oil and smear it on your face for a cheap, easy facial mask. Rinse off after a few minutes, just as the room is getting nice and steamy. Then for the best part: grab a magazine or juicy novel and just immerse yourself in a world of one. Soak as long as the water stays hot, and then, relaxed and restored, greet your returning family with a big smile on your face!

10. And Once a Year . . .

Try to work in a massage, even if it's a cheapie done by students of your local masseuse training center. You'll release toxins and relax muscles, and, well, you'll walk out of there as limp as a noodle and slightly high—in a good way! Ask for a massage for Christmas, your birthday, your anniversary, or Mother's Day, or just save up your "egg money" for that one blessed day of bliss. Sven would approve!

FUN THINGS

Sue tries to unwind, and you won't believe what happens.

One time I ordered a home waxing system from a TV shopping channel. I had been up late one night nursing my baby, and I was thinking I had let myself get kind of hairy since our family grew to four people. I was quite proud of my clever idea to order this kit instead of buying it in a store or going to a salon. After all, it's hard enough to get out to go grocery shopping, never mind to the beauty salon! Well, one night after I received the waxing kit in the mail, I put the kids to bed early and with great enthusiasm opened the box and got started with my "home salon." I melted the wax in the microwave, as the instructions said, and applied the warm goop on my armpits first. The directions said to keep my arms raised while the wax went to work on removing the hair.

So I was standing around in my underwear, arms raised, when I heard the dog barfing on our new carpet. My husband, Mike, was gone at a meeting, so I was the only one who could save the carpet. I ran to the living room and realized any one of my neighbors could see me in my bra and panties if they should happen to look in our window right then. So with arms still raised, I got down on my knees and kind of shuffled over to the kitchen cabinet that holds the special carpet cleaner and cleaning cloths. I realized I would have to put at least one arm down to clean the carpet, so I made the deadly error of doing so, not realizing how incredibly sticky the wax was. It also began to dawn on me that, in my haste to get the carpet cleaned, I had probably gone a few minutes over the suggested time for the wax application. I scrubbed the carpet the best I could with one arm and then tried to raise my arm again. Nope, wasn't happening. No matter how hard I tried to unstick my arm from my armpit, it wasn't budging. It was like cement or something—seriously!

Just as I was crawl-shuffling past the living room window again, Mike walked in the front door. "What are you doing?" he said, his eyes bugged out of his head. (To get a better visual, remember that I was in my underwear and shuffling on my knees with one hand raised.) Well, it was too much for me to take, and I started to cry. "I glued my armpit shut!" I bawled. "Sue," Mike said, looking truly concerned about the state of my mental health, "you have got to get out of the house more often!"

15

Ten Things the Best Moms Do

Working out the biggies

1. Control Your Anger

Who, me? Yeah, you, and me too. We would take a bullet for those precious kids of ours, but they still find ways to regularly make us nuts. Only our kids can so effectively stomp on our last nerves, at times leaving us unhinged, unglued, and unattached to our self-control and sanity. So we yell, we blow up, and we basically lose sight of the fact that a lot of the time, our children can't help it.

"In the deepest part of our mother brain, we know that 'kids will be kids,' that it's normal and even healthy for them to make mistakes and act immature and even get themselves into trouble," says Julie Barnhill, author of *She's Gonna Blow!*[1]

The best moms own this fact that our kids are going to irritate and frustrate us. But we also know we are works in progress. "I'm not perfect. I make lots of mistakes. There are times when my kids definitely drive me crazy," says Cheryl. "But I still love them, and I tell them so."

Work-in-progress moms pray for patience, identify the deeper things that trigger out-of-proportion anger, and try and try again to respond with control, calmness, and caring. And we work on accepting our imperfect kids. "Look your child squarely in the eye, and tenderly holding his face in your hands, say, 'I love you just the way you are!'" Julie writes. "Do it at least twice a week so that the reality of the message can sink into both your child's heart and your heart."[2]

2. When You Blow It, Ask for Forgiveness

"I've found myself apologizing to Ben for mistakes, freak-outs, etc." says Brenna. "I don't remember my parents ever apologizing to me! I'm trying to be real, mistakes and all." It's hard to kneel down and get face-to-face with a tearful little one, knowing full well he's crying because you snapped at him. "I'm sorry Mommy was grumpy with you just now, sweetie. Will you forgive me?" The healing begins at that moment, and the two of you can start fresh again. When you apologize, as Brenna does, you model how to do that very thing that's so hard to do, and you teach a priceless life skill in a world that hates to say, "I'm sorry."

3. Don't Attach Labels

"Jonah's the sports addict, and Ezra's our little artist." It's only human to want to "sort" your child's traits into recognizable file folders, isn't it? But the best moms avoid labeling their kids, especially with negative tags: "Quit being such a baby." "You've got to stop being such a bully to your baby sister!" "Creegan's so sensitive, aren't you, sweetie?"

Baby. Bully. Sensitive one. When we classify our kids in these ways, they take the labels to heart and begin to live up to or down to them. Aiden gets the message he's really a crybaby and therefore bawls at the drop of a hat. Brad begins to believe he can't help being mean to his sister or anyone else. And Creegan doesn't bother developing a thicker skin because, after all, he's the "sensitive one" in the family. I know one mom—a good one—who on a regular basis jokingly refers to her extremely strong-willed, active little boy as a "brat." Usually the comment is not directed at him, but he's within earshot anyway. Guess what? The kid *is* a brat, but reinforcing his behavior by labeling him thus only revs up his impish little engine.

A far better approach is to address the specific behavior and leave the adjectives about your child's personality out of it. For example, "Sydney's feelings were hurt when you grabbed her dolly. How can we make her feel better?"

"Even labels that seem neutral or positive—shy or smart—pigeonhole a child and place unnecessary or inappropriate expectations on her," says writer Paula Spencer.[3]

I've taken this to heart with my Ezra, who seems to display a real flair for art, although I may be biased. But I restrain myself from introducing him as "my extremely gifted child whom we refer to as 'the next Rembrandt.'" And instead of calling him "my little artiste," I try to say things like, "It's so fun that you enjoy painting and drawing so much."

4. Laugh

For a population subset who usually manages to ruin every punch line, preschoolers are a hilarious bunch. The best moms laugh a lot with (and sometimes at) their peculiar pint-sized comedians, who don't even have a clue how funny they are. Take time during your busy day to giggle. Enjoy your quirky preschooler because, trust me, they get less quirky as they grow up. How can you not get a kick out of a person who says, in all seriousness, "Mommy, you remind me of my imaginary friend from when I was a baby"?

"I feel one of the best things I do for Josephine is loving her and enjoying her so that she feels loved and enjoyed," says Mary Jo. "And talking to her a lot because she never stops talking to me!" Your undivided attention means the world to your kid—and we all love it when someone thinks we're funny, cute, and enjoyable!

5. Cry

Preschoolers shed many, many tears . . . still. We may be weary of mopping up one little emotional crisis after another, but the reality is that three- to five-year-olds are still at a tender stage in their development. Lots of blubbering, then, is to be expected. They still can't always verbalize what they're feeling, but when life frustrates, saddens, scares, or disappoints them, this age group will let it all hang out emotionally.

The best moms don't shut them down with a knee-jerk "Don't cry." We don't immediately deny that the child is frustrated, sad, scared, or disappointed. Obviously, the kid is feeling *something*. Instead, we offer hugs and tissues, and we help them acknowledge their emotions. "I know it's disappointing that we can't visit Nana right now, but we'll see her soon." Worried this plan will only encourage more weepiness? Actually, the opposite is true. "By naming the real feelings that your child has, you'll give him the words to express himself—and you'll show him what it means to be empathetic," says Paula Spencer. "Ultimately, he'll cry less and describe his emotions instead."[4]

6. Let It Go

"I have learned to laugh—even out loud!—at myself and at things that go awry around the house," says Ann. "I grew up with the notion that to be OK, you had to be perfect. I don't want to pass that on to my children, and I am trying hard to create a more realistic model of life." Life's messy, especially with small people who have a special talent for adding clutter, noise, and sometimes general mayhem to a household. Like Ann, the best moms learn to let go of the little, niggling things that get under their skin. Right now, as I gaze into my backyard filled with sticks, toys, and—arrgh!—even candy wrappers, I am itching to drop what I'm doing here, march outside, and demand the little litterbugs clean up *this instant*. However, I'm going to take a deep breath or two, make a mental note to calmly discuss

proper garbage disposal techniques and stick storage poli-
cies, and deal with the issue later on. What do you need to
let go of? I bet you'll easily think of some good examples
as you raise your stick-wielding, toy-overlooking, candy-
wrapper–dropping children!

7. Slow Down

It's just about impossible to rush small children, especially
those who have their own agenda. Actually, they all have
their own agendas. In our rush, rush, rush world, we moms
feel the need to hasten things along. Dabney can't find one
of her shoes? What else is new? You sigh, roll your eyes, and
scurry all over the house like the proverbial female poultry
with no head, trying to find the child's matching shoe. "We're
going to be late for the doctor," you screech. And the same
hurried, hectic scenario plays out every day.

This mom-rushing-poky-kids scenario is timeless. I recall
my dad telling me and my brother to "get a move on" or "shake
a leg" when we were being slowpokes. It's not 1976 anymore,
so I don't use those particular phrases when I'm prodding my
poky ones, but I do hiss, "Let's go!" and I do clap my hands
obnoxiously and bark, "Chop chop, people!" The effect is the
same: harried, resentful kids who just don't get what the big
heated rush is about. How do the best moms cope? By turning
down the exasperation and turning up the peace. Evaluate
your schedule to see if it's too packed. Toss whatever can go
in the "life's too short" pile of time consumers. Assess your
morning routine the night before. Collect Dabney's shoes—or
ask her to collect them herself—before bed that night so
there's no stressful scramble to find them as you're trying to

get out the door the next morning. And do be intentional about finding goodly amounts of time just to hang out with your child. After all, life shouldn't be all go, go, go.

"Instead of always trying to keep up with our hectic schedule, sometimes I take some time with Gabbi just to be together," says Jen T. "We'll have a picnic on my bed and recharge with a good little movie and some books to read together. Gabbi and I have been known to spend a whole afternoon together on my bed, and we both feel better afterward. I view this as our 'checkin' in time.' It's amazing what a few hours of real one-on-one time can do for future cooperation! When I am pushing her and she resists, I take it as a signal to just stop and take a breather."

8. Show Them the World

You may not be able to afford a family trip to Tonga, Madagascar, or Luxembourg, but you can definitely teach your kids about the big, bright, color-filled world they live in. We would love to bring our kids to Korea to see the country their baby sister is from. Maybe someday we will. But for now, we are drumming up enthusiasm for this exotic culture that's become so much a part of our family. We go to Korean restaurants, and although the kids don't order the fiery dishes that would make their eyes water, they do appreciate rice and sweet Korean barbecue. We've watched videos about the country, pointing out the tae kwon do to Jonah and the radiant celadon pottery to Ezra. We've flipped through photography books about the "hermit kingdom," and we are always on the lookout for children's books. The boys can both find Korea on the globe too.

You may not be adopting a baby from across the world, but you can impart a vision of how vast and interesting places are and how beautiful and different people are. To raise a child who appreciates this diversity, get her a globe or world-map puzzle and discuss other countries and places. You might need to do a little research yourself, but you needn't have all the answers. Grab a book about a different country each week when you visit the library, and check out ethnic restaurants. Think your kids would balk at African, Indian, or Middle Eastern food? They might, but cop a positive attitude and ease your way into it with, say, burritos at a Mexican restaurant or chicken fried rice at an Asian eatery. Frame these outings as adventures, and your enthusiasm just might be contagious.

You can also look up foreign-language kits for kids at your local bookstore. Since Jonah's been a toddler, we've listened to a Berlitz German-language tape with follow-along stories and songs. (My family speaks German, and when I was a little girl some of my first phrases were *auf Deutsch*. I wanted my kids to get a taste for their mother's "mother tongue.") Preschoolers are sponges when it comes to foreign language, and these tapes are easy to follow even if you don't know the language yourself. When you make an effort to spark interest about the world, you truly expand your child's horizons.

9. Practice Self-Care

Why are we moms so thick-skulled when it comes to taking care of our own needs? I've said it before, but I'll harangue you one more time: superior moms nurture themselves so they can better nurture their munchkins! "The best thing I can do as a mom for my children is take care of myself," says Ann. "When I eat well, sleep well, and get some exercise, I can cope better with the daily struggles of parenting preschoolers. I get out regularly with friends to refresh and recharge and go on regular dates with Dan." Sounds sensible to me. If the caregiver is cared for, she is that much more equipped not just to wipe noses, fix endless grilled cheese sandwiches, and find matching socks, but to do the harder emotional work of caring for the long haul.

Be on the lookout for ways to give yourself little boosts every day. And don't forget bigger, mommy-leaves-the-building refreshers either. My friend Emily can't wait for her next special outing. "I found this place that will do pedicures for twenty-two dollars," she raved. "I'm all about having my toes done once a month this year. This is definitely going to be the summer of my toes!"

10. The Best of the Best

Teaching your little one about the God who loves her and cares for her is by far the most vital and essential thing you can do as a mom. Doing so lays a moral foundation, answers her questions about the world, and models for her what it means to walk with God as she makes decisions. The best moms, including those of our preschool panel, make spirituality a core value in their mothering. "We try to instill in Grace that Christ loves her for who she is and that she should be proud of and love herself," says Christy. "Helping her to be a confident kid who loves the Lord is so important to our family."

The All-Time Best Entertainment Moms

Consider the matriarchs of television and the silver screen, the moms who, though not "real," contributed something to our understanding of motherhood, whether good or bad. The baddies, like Faye Dunaway in *Mommie Dearest*, showed us definitively how *not* to be moms.

But the best entertainment *madres* nurtured us somehow through the screen, sparking dreams, inspiring trust, and teaching us that mothers do hold up this world. Here are my top ten movie and TV mamas.

My Favorite

1. Lainie Kazan, *My Big Fat Greek Wedding* (2002)
   As she rolls dough for baklava, Toula's mama does not miss a beat. It's her warmth and instincts that keep the Greek clan from unraveling when their daughter brings home an outsider.

Classic Moms

2. Irene Dunne, *I Remember Mama* (1948)
   Have a mondo box of tissues on hand for this weepy film about an immigrant mama who guides her daughters in the new world.

3. Greer Garson, *Mrs. Miniver* (1942)
   The scene where Mom Miniver comforts her kids in

194

the bomb shelter as England is shelled in World War II makes a beeline for the old tear ducts.

4. Myrna Loy, *Cheaper by the Dozen* (1950)
   Forget the smarmy Ashton Kutcher remake and grab the funnier original featuring Loy as wife of efficiency expert Clifton Webb and mother of twelve.

Leave It to Beaver Moms

5. Barbara Billingsley as June Cleaver, *Leave It to Beaver* (1957–63)
   Ward and the Beav have Mom on the run, but she still manages to polish her floors in high heels and pearls.

6. Marion Ross as Marion Cunningham, *Happy Days* (1974–84)
   Mrs. C. always makes sure Joanie and Richie have their clothes ironed for the sock hop.

7. June Lockhart as Ruth Martin, *Lassie* (1958–64)
   That spunky collie always comes home to Timmy— and to Timmy's mom.

Fun Moms

8. Holly Hunter as Helen Parr, *The Incredibles* (2004)
   We think the whole turning-her-body-into-a-speedboat move is pretty fun, don't you?

9. Lucille Ball, *I Love Lucy* (1951–57)

Squishing a vat of grapes with her bare feet, speed-eating chocolates as they come down the assembly line . . . we could go on, but suffice it to say little Ricky never has a dull moment with his caper-happy mom.

10. Shirley Jones as Shirley Partridge, *The Partridge Family* (1970–74)

Ma Partridge brings home the bacon, fries it up in a pan, and plays keyboard in her family's garage band. How cool is that?

Preschoolers have such earnest little hearts! They are the anticynics, the wide-eyed wonder boys and girls who regard God and his beauty and mystery with the awe he deserves. "I'm trying to teach them about Jesus and the love he has for them. We pray before meals, read Bible stories, and talk about what it means to be a Christian—loving God, others, and yourself," says Kim.

Now is the time to plant those seeds of faith in your children's tender souls. There simply won't be a better time in their lives to shape their view of the world and God, and this unjaded openness won't last forever. A wise grandpa once told his daughter to stop and listen to her kids when they were small, while they were clamoring for her attention and bursting with stories, jokes, and even grumbles. "If you listen to them when they're little," he said, "your kids will listen to you when they're older." Listen to the endless questions and answer them, praying for wisdom and guidance. The best moms do, and it pays off for all eternity.

And Before We Say, "See Ya" . . .

I just want to say thank you for riding along with me as we explored our beautiful, silly, wide-eyed wonder boys and girls. It's been more fun and meaningful for me than I ever could have imagined, and I hope and pray you've enjoyed it half as much as I have. These two years are something, aren't they? As my Ez the Pez creeps toward turning five, I realize again how rich and precious the preschool years are and how much I look forward to experiencing all of it again with baby Phoebe. I can't wait to hear your stories about your one-of-a-kind preschooler! May you hug your little one more tightly, laugh louder at his or her hilarious ways, and most important, see the world as being more amazing and marvelous through his or her awe-filled eyes.

FUN THINGS

A final few *bons mots* from the mouths of babes at preschool

Micah (after buttoning his pants): "Oh, we need to zip the barn door!"

Noah: "God, thank you for this day. And thank you for bringing all these precious children here today."

Sam (after drawing a lion picture): "These are two boys. They are eating cantaloupe [antelope] on the beach."

197

Student teacher to Nathan: "How would you feel if you were walking next to an adult rhino?"

Nathan: "If you were in your car, you would be kind of angry, because it would knock down your car. And that would not be very nice of the rhino!"

Noel: "Here's your invitation to mine and Bastiaan's wedding!"

Baldwin: "Hey, people, Jesus loves you guys!"

Kross: "My dad makes noises when he sleeps."
Miss Jessie: "What do you call that?"
Kross: "An elephant."

Acacia: "Old MacDonald's isn't healthy for you."

Isaiah (his eleventh commandment): "Do not eat the cake before it's ready!"

Justin K. (his eleventh commandment): "Do not break anyone else's heart."

Notes

Introduction

1. Paul C. Reisser, Melissa R. Cox, and Vinita Hampton Wright, *The Focus on the Family Complete Book of Baby and Child Care* (Wheaton: Tyndale House Publishers, 1997), 367.

Chapter 2 To Share Is Human

1. Marisa Cohen, "Preschool Teacher Advice," *Parents*, November 2004, 90, www.parents.com/articles/age/5840.jsp.

2. Jessica Snyder Sachs, "Getting Kids to Get Along," *Parenting*, April 2003, 136.

Chapter 3 "If You're Going to Kill Each Other, Do It in the Basement!"

1. Kevin Leman, *Making Children Mind without Losing Yours* (Grand Rapids: Revell, 1984), 179.

2. Ibid.

3. Anthony E. Wolf, "Peace at Last," *Parenting*, September 2003, 118.

4. Ibid.

Chapter 4 Beyond Cereal, Grilled Cheese, and PB&J

1. Lawrence Kutner, "Taming the Picky Eater," © 1998, All About Moms, www.allaboutmoms.com.

2. Ibid.

3. Ibid.

4. Leman, *Making Children Mind*, 179.

5. "Ways to Get Picky Eaters to Eat," Parent Soup Problem Solvers, 2004, www.americasbest.com/Babies/Parenting/parentsoup.htm.

6. William Sears, "Healthy Eating," *Parenting*, November 2003, 117.

Chapter 5 Mommy's Going to the Mat!

1. Valerie Frankel, "Teaching Choices," *Parenting*, October 2002, 121.

2. Michael de Jong, "The Power of Imagination: The Role of Dress-Up Play in Child Development," Small Miracles, Inc., 2004, http://preschoolers.com.

Chapter 6 Things That Go Bump in the Night

1. William Sears, "Boogeyman Blues," *Parenting*, May 2004, 43.

2. "Can You Help?" *Parents*, September 2003, 20.

Chapter 7 Gets and Goodness

1. Diane Harris, "My Kids, Money and Me," *Parenting*, September 2003, 223.

2. Mary M. Byers, *The Mother Load: How to Meet Your Own Needs While Caring for Your Family* (Eugene, OR: Harvest House, 2005), 112.

3. Harris, "My Kids, Money and Me," 223.

4. John W. Lee, "On the Fast Track: The Appeal of Wooden Train Play," http://preschoolers.com.

Chapter 8 "Please Unclamp Yourself from My Leg"

1. Suzanne Dixon, M.D., M.P.H., "Stressed-Out Kids," http://pampers.com.

Chapter 9 "Whack the Piñata, Not the Cake!"

1. Shelly Radic, personal interview.

2. Erika Stremler Pott, personal interview.

Chapter 10 Extreme Granny Makeover

1. Susan Newman, quoted in Kellye Carter Crocker, "Annoying Little Grandparent Problems," *Parents*, November 2004, 60.

Chapter 11 "Can We Talk?"

1. Byers, *Mother Load*, 47.
2. Carmen Renee Berry and Tamara Traeder, *Girlfriends: Invisible Bonds, Enduring Ties* (Tulsa: Wildcat Canyon Press, 1998), 60.
3. John W. Lee, "Valuable Life Lessons," 2004, http://preschoolers.com.
4. Ibid.
5. Byers, *Mother Load*, 47.
6. Angela Thomas Gruffy, *Tender Mercy for a Mother's Soul* (Wheaton, Tyndale, 2001), 192.

Chapter 12 Mom and Dad Got It Goin' On

1. Michele Weiner Davis, quoted in Trish Thompson, "A Little Romance," *Parenting*, March 2005, 129.
2. "Naked in Front of the Kids?" *Parenting*, 2004, http://www.parenting.com.

Chapter 13 Like the Skin You're In

1. Debra Waterhouse, *Outsmarting the Female Fat Cell—After Pregnancy: Every Woman's Guide to Shaping Up, Slimming Down, and Staying Sane After the Baby* (New York: Hyperion, 2002), 30.

Chapter 14 Mommy Minispas

1. Byers, *Mother Load*, 9.

Chapter 15 Ten Things the Best Moms Do

1. Julie Barnhill, *She's Gonna Blow!* (Eugene, OR: Harvest House, 2005), 9.
2. Ibid.
3. Paula Spencer, "9 Things You Shouldn't Say to Your Child," *Parenting*, 2004, www.parenting.com.
4. Ibid.

ACKNOWLEDGMENTS

My humble gratitude to the following people:

To Abe and Linda Reimer, Dan and Tina Reimer, Ken and Linda Craker, Mike and Jodi Connell, Lorraine and Tracy Bush, and George and Pat Vanderlaan for family support. A special thanks to Mom C for taking care of the boys during the deadline crunch for this book!

To pals Bonnie Anderson, Nancy Rubin, Peggy Anderson, Becky Wertz Walker, Lisa Freire, Carla Klassen, Kathy Graffam, Stephanie Nelson, Sheri Rodriguez, Rachel Vanderlaan Arnold, and Juliana Clink for general girlfriend-ish support.

To my beautiful writer's guild ladies, Ann Byle, Julie Johnson, Angela Blyker, Tracy Groot, Jen Abbas, and Shelly Beach, for encouragement, laughs, and for understanding about book deadlines, agents, and all that jazz.

To the Baker Publishing Group gang, especially Mary Wenger, Dwight Baker, and Paula Gibson, for being great to work with!

To Twila Bennett, marketing manager and friend extraordinaire. See you at the next Tim McGraw show! Maybe we'll even get to hang out with McMahon again.

To Jennifer Leep, a fabulous editor. Thanks, Jen, for all your support, encouragement, and good guidance.

And finally, to my family, Doyle, Jonah, Ezra, and Phoebe—I love you very much. Special thanks to Jonah and Ezra for having such vivid preschool daze!

Lorilee Craker speaks for MOPS groups and at other events for mothers. She writes on entertainment for a major daily newspaper and is the author of four books including *A Is for Adam: Biblical Baby Names* and *O for a Thousand Nights to Sleep*. She lives in Grand Rapids, Michigan, with her husband, Doyle, and their two sons and a daughter.

About MOPS

You take care of your children, Mom. Who takes care of you? MOPS® International (Mothers of Preschoolers) provides mothers of preschoolers with the nurture and resources they need to be the best moms they can be.

MOPS is dedicated to the message that "mothering matters" and that moms of young children need encouragement during these critical and formative years. Chartered groups meet in approximately four thousand churches and Christian ministries throughout the United States and in thirty other countries. Each MOPS program helps mothers find friendship and acceptance, provides opportunities for women to develop and practice leadership skills in the group, and promotes spiritual growth. MOPS groups are chartered ministries of local churches and meet at a variety of times and locations: daytime, evenings, and on weekends; in churches, homes, and workplaces.

The MOPPETS program offers a loving, learning experience for children while their moms attend MOPS. Other MOPS resources include *MOMSense®* magazine and radio, the MOPS International website, and books and resources available through the MOPShop.

With 14.3 million mothers of preschoolers in the United States alone, many moms can't attend a local MOPS group. These moms still need the support that MOPS International can offer! For a small registration fee, any mother of preschoolers can join the MOPS♥to♥Mom Connection® and receive *MOMSense* magazine six times a year, a weekly Mom-E-Mail message of encouragement, and other valuable benefits.

Find out how MOPS International can help you become part of the MOPS♥to♥Mom Connection and/or join or start a MOPS group. Visit our website at www. MOPS.org. Phone us at 303-733-5353. Or email Info@ MOPS.org. To learn how to start a MOPS group, call 1-888-910-MOPS.

More Inspiration

Five-Star Families

★★★★★

MOVING YOURS FROM
GOOD TO GREAT

Carol Kuykendall

dollars & sense

a mom's guide to
money matters

finding strategies
that work for you
& your family

cynthia sumner

Take a Break From Your *Wipe-a-Nose* Workday

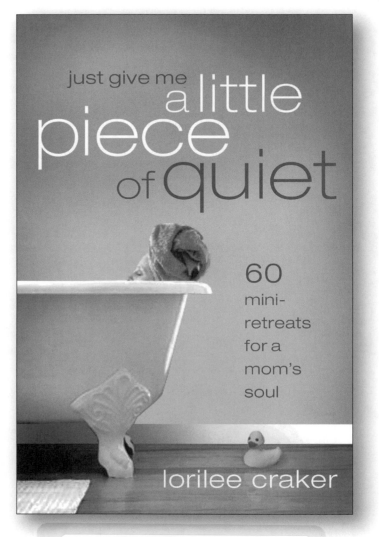

just give me **a little**
piece
of **quiet**

60
mini-
retreats
for a
mom's
soul

lorilee craker

Available at your loca